QUEEN ANNE
&
GEORGIAN
LOOKING
GLASSES

CHIPPENDALE PARCEL-GILDED WALNUT PIER MIRROR. Expertized as *ENGLISH*, as *AMERICAN*, and as *AMERICAN OR ENGLISH*. Actually an unmistakable metropolitan design, clearly originating in the long overlooked (or intentionally ignored) principal furniture center of Dublin during that capital's greatest period of productivity.

QUEEN ANNE & GEORGIAN LOOKING GLASSES

F. LEWIS HINCKLEY

WITH SUPPLEMENT ON THE DISTRIBUTORS OF
COLONIAL AND EARLY FEDERAL LOOKING GLASSES

322 ILLUSTRATIONS

THE TAURIS
ANTIQUES PRESS
London

Published in 1990 by
The Tauris Antiques Press
110 Gloucester Avenue
London NW1 8JA

Copyright © 1987 by F. Lewis Hinckley

All rights reserved. Except for brief quotations in a review, this book, or any part thereof, must not be reproduced in any form without permission in writing from the publisher.

British Library Cataloguing in Publication Data
Hinckley, F. Lewis
   Queen Anne and Georgian looking glasses.
   I. Title
   747.9

ISBN 1-85043-253-8

Manufactured in the United States of America.

Dedicated to
F. ROY STAMP (Biggs of Maidenhead),
one of the earliest contributors to these researches;
and to
REGINALD LUMB (Charles Lumb & Sons),
one of the latest;
both being especially appreciative
of Dublin's designs in her originally
untaxed looking glasses,
as thus so widely distributed
throughout the British Isles
and to America,
during the eighteenth century.

Contents

Foreword	1
The Comparative Proving System	3
The Importance of Looking Glasses	7
The Development of Dublin Looking Glasses	9
Distributors of Colonial and Early Federal Looking Glasses	21
Addendum	24
Plates	27
Index	251

Foreword

ACCORDING TO THE JUDGMENTS of all accepted authorities on Old English and Early American Furniture the following masterpieces of Queen Anne and Georgian looking glasses, in their entirety, are either "English" or "American." Therefore it would have been extremely unwise for any of the more knowledgeable English and American professional antique dealers represented here to dispute those judgments or the misleading systems of classification that have come into effect through their complete acceptance by English and American museums, lay writers, and consequently, collectors at large.

A debt of gratitude on the part of all those who would know about, and wish to identify the actual source of the most admired Queen Anne and Georgian looking glasses, according to the developing styles and their thoroughly distinctive designs, so amply covered in the following illustrations, is therefore owed each contributor to this work for now permitting publication of the most representative examples in accordance with their true prestigious capital city origins.

The Comparative Proving System

As the first scientific investigation

of

Queen Anne and Georgian Furniture

SOME TIME AFTER the fourth Duke of Beaufort (Charles Noel 1705-1736) had completed the furnishing of his famous Chinese-Chippendale Bedroom in Badminton House, Gloucestershire, with pieces obtained from nearby Dublin, that residence was visited by a Doctor Pocock who later described the room in Volume II of his *Travels Through England*, which was published in 1754*.

In consideration of the time required for the completion of Doctor Pocock's travels, for the preparation of his book, and for its publication, it is clear that the Duke must have ordered his bedroom furniture well before the publication, also in 1754, of Thomas Chippendale's first *Director*. Thus it is evident that the Duke's famous bedstead, now a Museum Acquisition rightly described as *one of the most successful examples of the Chinese Vogue*, was designed and executed in Dublin without any possible assistance from Chippendale or his first *Director*.

Indeed with the Chippendale style thus so firmly established in Dublin at least by 1750, it might be that Chippendale was just as well acquainted with those developments in the Irish capital, as he was with the Parisian designs of Juste-Aurele Meissonier, which he was not above presenting as his own.

The diagonal open-fret pattern of the Badminton bedstead's four large latticework panels appears in small-scale patterns of chairs, tables and cabinets produced during the following years. However, the clustered ribbings encircled by floretted ties, on the front and rear tall posts, are most unusual. That is also true of the somewhat similar treatments appearing on the back uprights, front seat rail and legs of the Dublin settee formerly owned by Governor Wentworth of New Hampshire. This was confiscated and sold by the federal government in 1776. Although variously dated as *circa 1760-1765*, and *circa 1770*, comparisons with other Chippendale designs produced during those years will not reveal any evidence in dispute of a more accurate dating of *circa* 1750, as substantiated by the design and execution of the Badminton bedstead.

---

*Edwards and Jourdain, *Georgian Cabinet-Makers*, (London, 1955), p. 70.

Not only in such separate instances of Chippendale furniture arriving in America, but also in regard to the Queen Anne and Georgian wall mirrors received in Early American homes during the Colonial and Early Federal years, virtually all of such importations were obtained from Dublin, rather than London. In fact preferences for Dublin, rather than London designs, in furniture and looking glasses, still prevail in the repeated popularity, with present-day American collectors, of all such antique masterpieces for their superior decorative values in the furnishing of contemporary interiors.

Despite that current popularity, American collectors have still to realize the extent to which so-called Old English Furniture is comprised mainly of fine, imaginatively designed, but entirely unrecognized Dublin masterpieces, having very little or nothing to do with the designs of authentic London productions. This is especially true of most London pieces, obviously made for royalty and the nobility, and which in any case are seldom permitted to enter the public market.

In a first attempt to illustrate furniture designed and executed only by known London craftsmen, the leading English museum and literary authorities, Ralph Edwards and Margaret Jourdain, in their *Georgian Cabinet-Makers* gathered together an unimpressive number of such authentic palatial masterpieces. Intermixed with these, other masterpieces shown as at Badminton, Kimbolton Castle, Nostel Priory, etc., and mistakenly attributed to William Vile or Thomas Chippendale, are more appealing to present-day tastes in home furnishings because of their more engaging Dublin designs.

None of the pieces illustrated in that work, or in any other London publications as in, at or from Badminton House, Gloucestershire, were received there from London. This includes a Chippendale overmantel mirror illustrated, Fig. 8, in Percy Macquoid's *Age of Satinwood*, which matches the Badminton bedstead.

That mirror helped in confirming the same Dublin origin for a Museum Acquisition published many years ago in the *Connoisseur* as a "Mirror. Carved Wood Frame with Lacquer Decoration in the "Chinese" Rococo Style. German; About 1740. H. 8 ft. 9 in. Bought Out of the Funds of the Murray Bequest."

It is not surprising for such a fanciful masterpiece to be so described, for in their failures to "see the forest for the trees" in respect to the preponderance of Dublin productions *vis-à-vis* the relatively small number of pieces that are actually provable as *bona fide* London productions, English authorities have also been inclined to misinterpret some of the unrecognized Dublin creations as *German*, though more frequently they have been accepted as *Dutch*.

An allegation that any of the individual features of the Badminton bedstead might have been copied in some other production at some other time, brought to mind as an especially disproving example, that particular "German" Museum Acquisition. Aside from its features paralleling those of the Badminton overmantel, its dragon finials, clearly unmatched in any other Georgian (or German) production from about 1750 or later, make it, also, virtually *en suite* with the Badminton bedstead.

Such Museum Acquisitions have been especially serviceable to these particular researches. It has been found that in the relative scarcity of authentic London masterpieces, English museum officials have been apt to look upon every recently imported Dublin masterpiece of Queen Anne or Georgian furniture as another possibility for increasing that remarkably small representation of *bona fide* London productions.

The Comparative Proving System

The one infallible method through which the true origin of such new arrivals in the London antique market might have been determined, is to subject every such example to an exhaustive comparative study of its design in relation to all other clearly related Queen Anne or Georgian examples. This of course would be impractical without instant access to all pertinent examples of so-called Old English Furniture illustrated throughout the present century. It is obvious that no such truly scientific research has ever been carried out in Great Britain, where attributions have always been based upon extended deliberative judgments, opinions, beliefs or other forms of theoretical guesswork, as indulged in by even the most highly regarded English literary and museum authorities.

Recent improvements in making photocopies of halftone illustrations make it no longer necessary to obtain all possible illustrations necessary to build up such a comparative proving system by removing them from books, magazines, museum bulletins, auction catalogues, etc. in which they have appeared. This was an expensive as well as a destructive process when the present researches were initiated, and for many years after, especially when it came to taking apart three- and four-volume works such as the *Dictionary of English Furniture* and Percy Macquoid's *Ages*. Today, however, such an excessive process is no longer necessary, or even feasible, since illustrations on both sides of a page may now be photocopied without any such overpage losses.

With a nucleus of such halftone illustrations the construction of an easily workable comparative proving system also requires its amplification by photographs of as many additional design-related examples as may prove helpful in substantiating, or in finally confirming, the designs of these, or other examples awaiting such additional proofs of their correct origin. Present-day costs of photographs and photographic prints, will make it unlikely that any such fully expanded research project will ever again be undertaken by a private individual.

It is only through this first scientific proving method in its application to Dublin *vis-à-vis* London furniture, that the very latest of Museum Acquisitions, such as the recently publicized Channon and Langlois Pieces, and Weekes' Museum Cabinets, will eventually become recognizable to English museum authorities as being thoroughly characteristic Dublin creations having absolutely nothing whatsoever in common with any authentic London productions.

This may not occur before the designs of Dublin furniture and looking glasses have first become more generally obvious to American collectors, who are unlikely to be enduringly impressed by the efforts of the London Publishing Industry toward a strict maintenance of the *status quo*. This by a continuous flow of books supposedly concentrated solely on the best selling subject of Old *English* Furniture, but which instead are liberally illustrated with unrecognized masterpieces originating in the persistently ignored Irish capital. This also despite the fact that after only Paris and London, Dublin was formerly the third-largest capital of the Western world; the only one whose fine and superfine furniture has not received worldwide recognition in the museum exhibits and literature of the last hundred years.

The Importance of Looking Glasses

In widening the distribution
of
Queen Anne and Georgian Furniture

FROM LONDON'S COMPARATIVELY remote position in the far southeastern corner of the British Isles, it was decidedly handicapped in the distribution of Queen Anne and Georgian furniture in relation to the geographical situation of Dublin, which lay in the very heart of that community. This placed the second capital in relatively close proximity to all western counties of England, Scotland and Wales, which could be reached from London only by ten days to two weeks or more of sailing time.

Further disadvantages were introduced by the British government itself in the Excise Act of 1745, which levied such exorbitant duties on all English glass that trade in such articles was largely diverted to Dublin, a tax-free port and principal market for all types of Queen Anne and Georgian looking glasses. A following Act doubled even those excessive duties, with repercussions again so distressful that for the second time glassworks in London and its environs were forced to shut down and glassmakers there were obliged to seek employment in Dublin and Waterford.

By those decrees the administration in London had also raised the importance of Dublin in respect to its production of seat furniture and cabinetwork as well as that of looking glasses and their frames. One cannot imagine that either the Scots and Welsh, or the well-to-do English, in their purchases of fine looking glasses, would willingly pay excessive amounts for these in the highly taxed and seriously diminished London market, especially when they could be bought far more advantageously in the amply supplied Dublin market. Then after any additional selections of Dublin or Waterford chandelieres, girandoles, candelabra, etc., they would have two alternatives. With continued ease and availability they could decide right then and there on any requirements in seat furniture and cabinetwork, of styles and designs in conformity with those of the mirrors just ordered. Or, on the speculative possibility that such requirements might be as plentifully available in the English capital, they could undergo the time and trouble and additional expense involved in a further journey to London to find out.

The latter alternative would have appealed to few of even the most affluent visitors, according to all remaining evidence. A good proportion of the most important British homes, including some lying less than a hundred miles from the English capital, are still equipped with their originally supplied Dublin mirrors and other furniture, as well as Waterford lighting fixtures, chosen in preference to any of somewhat similar furnishings that might have been available in London.

An instance of such partiality that has served these researches almost from their inception is Badminton House, in Gloucestershire, in which its famous Chinese-Chippendale bedroom was furnished by the Duke of Beaufort with such Dublin masterpieces of both furniture and looking glasses. These have all, nevertheless, been attributed by leading English museum and other lay authorities to London manufactures, and of course to Thomas Chippendale[1] (including its highly publicized bedstead, *vide* 219). This was described in 1754 by a Doctor Pocock in his *Travels Through England*. Since the first edition of Chippendale's *Director* did not appear until that same year, it should be plain that London could offer no real competition in such Chinese-Chippendale themes; the Duke's possessing a copy of Chippendale's *Director* does *not* constitute evidence of his work, and is acceptable as such only to those optimistic lay authorities.

The year 1754 is therefore an approximate date also of the Chinese-Chippendale settee formerly belonging to Governor Wentworth of New Hampshire, now on exhibition in Williamsburg. The design is actually *en suite* with the Badminton bedstead, though more elaborate than that of the chairs made for the Duke. The presence of such a masterpiece in America cannot, however, be taken as proof that Dublin seat furniture was imported here to any particular extent, for American furniture craftsmen were well able to meet all such demands. Requirements that could not be fulfilled in this country, but which were continuously supplied from Dublin and Waterford, were looking glasses, girandole mirrors, coach glasses, table glasswares, chandelieres[2] and other glass lighting fixtures. All of these continued to be received in America in ever increasing supplies throughout the balance of the eighteenth century and the later Georgian years.

---

1. Edwards & Jourdain, *Georgian Cabinet-Makers* (London, 1955), pp. 28, 70-71.
2. According to Derek C. Davis, specializing in *English and Irish Antique Glass* (1964), pp. 118-120, "The early chandelieres were, at first, simply constructed and were merely composed of six or seven ball-shaped hollow stem pieces on a metal rod above the circular arm plate with two or three sections below it and a ball or tapering shaped finial. Usually, six or eight gracefully designed 'S'-shaped candle arms slotted into the arm plate and all the fitments were hung with large single pear-shaped drops, each one being cut in perfect geometric and prismatic patterns. This type was in vogue about 1770 and most of them were being made in Ireland." After describing those of the Regency era he states that "All these types of chandelieres up till 1825 were made in Ireland, which has profited by the great boon of Free Trade and the immigration of many English craftsmen to escape the severe excise duties on raw materials in England. Drops, however, were ordered from England by several Irish makers."

The Development of Dublin Looking Glasses

THE COLORED GLASS WINDOWS of Dublin Castle are said to have been made in that city as early as 1332. Window glass, colored glass in various forms and drinking glasses of different types were produced there and elsewhere in Ireland during the sixteenth century. Domestic glass of every description was made in Dublin from the late seventeenth century on. This manufacture was increased as that of London diminished, and with free trading rights granted by the English government there was an added asset of wide export throughout the British Isles, to America and even to northern Europe. Little wonder, then, that looking glasses removed from or still remaining in Irish castles and mansions are entirely of native manufacture, with never a record of such mirrors and their frames, along with furniture in general, ever having been ordered or received from London—*i.e.* England as a whole—throughout Queen Anne and Georgian times.

A leading authority on the subject, Tennyson Little, has noted that Irish glass was exported in

> vast quantities to America, the West Indies, and even to England itself.... The output of Waterford was enormous, some idea of the magnitude of the work is given by the fact that up to 1820 some 200 craftsmen were employed daily in the glasshouse. By 1786 almost incredible amounts of glass were being exported to America, and it is recorded that in a mere two years, apart from other glassware, 100,382 drinking glasses were sent to New York alone.

Waterford glass chandelieres still remain in Trinity Church, New York, and in Independence Hall, Philadelphia. The glasses for coaches and chariots, as advertised by the Elliotts of Philadelphia, were obtained from the Irish capital, and the carriages themselves are recorded as arriving here from Dublin. Much of the Irish glass was in color, Dublin glass in particular showing rich shades of green, blue and amber.

Mirror glasses were costly, often far more so than their frames, which, to suit a later type of decor, might be made over as successfully as possible (*vide* 256); an old frame might be entirely discarded and the mirror plate supplied with a new frame designed for its reuse. For economy two sections of mirror plate were often used in tall frames when the uppermost would appear above eye level; this might be cut in scroll patterns, a star, coronet, etc. Chippendale frames might be fashioned with multiple shaped mirror panels or similar bordering effects, enclosing conformingly cut sections of mirror plate, thus reducing the cost of the principal reflecting surface. Later frames were also designed with a similar economy in mind.

The beauty and value of antique wall mirrors are in large part represented by their original mercury-back mirror plates. In fact, their loss in value through breakage has generally been accepted in insurance claims as amounting to a 50 percent decrease in that of the remaining frame with a replacement glass, preferably cut from a Victorian mercury-back mirror plate. Their rich and soft deep toned reflections are not due to the use of mercury but to that of lead in the glass itself.

Much has been said about the relative thinness of old mirror plates in comparison with those of Victorian and more recent times. In differing with these published opinions, I sought confirmation of my own findings through entirely qualified professionals. Mr. L. P. Lizotte, of Lizotte Glass, Holyoke, Massachusetts, has determined through his caliper measuring of antique mercury-back mirror plates that their thicknesses vary from 1/8 to 5/16 of an inch; he found similar measurements in later, Victorian mercury-back mirror plates. Entirely modern mirror plates may be even thinner, varying from only 1/16 to 1/4 of an inch.

The backings of these old and modern mirror plates (and the reason for the changeover in their compositions) have been accounted for by Mr. Morris Fox, of the Metropolitan Mirror and Glass Company in Mount Vernon, New York:

> "We do know that mercury backing was used in the manufacture of mirrors by our own Company until approximately 1908 or 1910. At that time it was discovered that the men in the silvering room were actually absorbing mercury into their systems with very harmful effects. Laws were passed which forbid the use of mercury in the silvering of mirrors. Accordingly the industry switched over to silver nitrate as a substitute solution for silvering, and this has been in use ever since. Instead of the silver tone appearing on the reverse of old mirror plates, the modern process results in one not too unlike a deep Sheraton-pink staining wash, or a copper back as noted along with 'Electro Copper Plated' in the present trademark of this company."

Heraldic bearings of various descriptions were popular in Dublin looking glass plates and frames. The example in tortoiseshell with royal British lion-and-unicorn (2) is a characteristic early type of design, but though it comes from an internationally known firm it is not a period piece. Crowns and coronets abound, carved or inlaid, sometimes with a monogram, or sometimes engraved in the rear surfaces of mirror plates before silvering.

Just as Holland is credited with furniture designs and working techniques never carried out or indeed never permitted in that country, various types of Dublin looking glasses are guessed at by unprofessional authorities as originating there. The cushion-molded marquetry frames (5 and 6) do bear some relationship to the frieze of the marquetry fall-front cabinet (7), but while this too has been authoritatively labeled as "Dutch," none of these pieces could have been made in Holland or elsewhere than in Dublin, the usual overlooked source of so many supposedly Dutch masterpieces.

The flat-arched heading of (14) appears also in a Dublin dressing mirror owned by Viscountess Wolseley (Macquoid, Fig. 154) and in another owned by Percival Griffiths (*Dictionary of English Furniture*, Fig. 15); both display identifying details similar to others in the elegant lady's dressing and writing table (48) authoritatively credited to a London maker long departed prior to its actual date of execution.

Where the immediately following glasses have been included in known collections or shipments of British furniture, they have been credited as "English." Where there has been no such information regarding a possible attribution, they might be offered as "American" or even as having originated in Massachusetts (16) or in Boston (17). In addition to the cut patterns of upper mirror plates, the spirited lacquer treatments are also typical of Dublin skills in this technique. These skills are enlarged upon in the three cabinet pieces (22, 23 and 24). The chest section of the latter example, the type erroneously associated with the reign of Charles II, is indicated as a much later, Georgian production by its interior structural features, and the original stand with carving somewhat similar to that employed in fashioning some of the over elaborated Irish side tables.

The Chippendale mirror (10) has been included as an instance of a graved upper and plain lower mirror plate in a frame of circa 1755 or later. As this came into the American market many years ago and I have not personally examined it, the possibility of reused plates, as previously mentioned, is certainly to be kept in mind.

Dublin origins are indicated by the pronounced structural features, distinctive inlays and lacquer decorations of the Queen Anne and Georgian dressing mirrors and slant-front desks (35 through 42). The design of (41) is almost exactly the same as a mahogany example labeled by John Elliott of Philadelphia (*vide* A Directory of the Historic Cabinet Woods, p. 114).

American walnut appears as a choice selection in some drawer linings of those dressing mirrors, and they may be fitted together with very delicate corner shims. While it has seldom been suggested as an indication of American origin in such instances, it is common practice for the presence of North American pine to be offered in that light with pier mirrors such as (148-168), etc. The cores of Dublin mirror frames, veneered or lacquered, and their backboards in particular, are often of such pine, American or Canadian: *Pinus abies* or spruce fir, the white variety botanically known as *Abies alba*, the black as *Abies nigra*. A yellow pine, *Pinus strobus*, also called American white pine, was introduced commercially at the beginning of the nineteenth century, when it is said to have almost entirely superceded the other varieties. I have traced eighteenth-century shipments of timbers in respect only to Philadelphia. However, since they were indigenous from Virginia to Canada and are recorded as having been received in great quantities, especially in Liverpool, they were readily available throughout the entirety of the British Isles. In this respect London, as generally supposed, was not the one great center of supply for the woodworking trades. Aside from those shipments known to have been directly received in Dublin, others were collected in large quantities just across the Irish Sea in Liverpool, which no doubt was more dependent on Dublin than London for the continuously increased prosperity of this trade that attracted Continental buyers as well.

Should these North American pines returned here in manufactured form be free of knots, this has been pointed out as additional evidence that the American craftsman had available such an abundant supply of framing and backing material that he could reject all but knot-free wood. Whenever such selectivity may indeed be encountered it would not have resulted from such a discarding, but from the Dublin frame maker's option, at only a small extra cost, of choosing his own planks individually, rather than buying them as they lay in the woodyard.

Just as the designs of Dublin furniture might in some instances postdate those of style developments in the English capital, so did those of Philadelphia and other American towns, in regard to which there could be an even greater time lapse before certain influences were transmitted here from overseas. Wall mirrors imported here from Dublin and today considered as Queen Anne in style are usually labelled as "American or English, *circa* 1730-1750," or even "*circa* 1740-1770." Avoiding the use of British terminology, later parcel-gilded walnut or mahogany mirror frames become "Chippendale" rather than Early Georgian, Georgian or Late Georgian.

Aside from the supposition that these looking glasses arrived in quantity from England despite the lack of any such trade, or that they were produced in American manufactories that simply did not exist, these design classifications are acceptable here as in conformity with those adopted in reference to American floor furniture in general. Of greater import is the fact that with more evidence forthcoming the *circa* dates arrived at here by professionally trained experts in Americana will prove to be more accurate than those surmised in regard to related Dublin examples delivered throughout the British Isles during the same above mentioned periods of time.

Looking glasses imported by John Elliott and his son were advertised as reaching Philadelphia in "vessels from London." They were not claimed as ordered from or made in that city, to which no comparable designs can be traced. It is unacceptable that thrifty American ship masters or supercargoes could be induced to pay excessive prices for highly—even doubly—taxed looking glasses in the London market, when they could be bought so much more economically in Dublin, where they were tax-free. The same would have been true had such manufactures been obtainable elsewhere in England, where other towns, however, were no further advanced than Philadelphia in their manufacturing capacities. Finally, it would have been impossible for the Elliotts' to carry on successfully both wholesale and retail businesses under their claim that they sold "Looking-glasses at the lowest Rates" had these been obtained at the highest possible rates; while their competitors and private clientele could do better by far in the leading British glass and looking-glass market.

An early type of mirror sold by John Elliott, such as his labeled pier mirror in the Metropolitan Museum, is closely related in design to others with similarly restrained summital scrolls centering Prince-of-Wales plumes, a favorite device of Dublin's mirror-frame makers, as well as her joiners and cabinetmakers, but hardly popular with all of the American colonists. In these frames the upper portion of the molding that surrounds the mirror plate is shaped as in (28, 29 and 32), a heading favored in mirrors supported on the highest quality Dublin dressing bureaus of the general form shown here, (42).

With the architecturally treated Elliott imports, the mirror plate is enclosed by an echinus molding, sometimes with flat-arched heading surmounted by a distinctive phoenix or Ho-Ho, with lateral open-work pendants of scrolling stems with leafage, blossoms and fruit, or fruit clusters, (158, 161, 162, etc). The same type of side pendants appears also in a well publicized overmantel of supposedly English origin (*Dictionary of English Furniture*, Fig. 43) with a "wooded landscape, painted in the Dutch manner," a misconception in keeping with those advanced so frequently in respect to Dublin furniture. The pedimental scrolls and their terminals in some of these architecturally treated frames match exactly those of other Dublin examples with bird-on-bough finials (178, 179, etc.).

The stand of the small piece (36), with desk section as that of the preceding dressing mirror may have prompted its misjudgment as Dutch. As usual, this could have resulted only from a lack of knowledge in that field, as well as that of Dublin furniture *per se* and therefore of Georgian furniture in general. In addition to the treatment of the drawer front, the sland lid features one of the most characteristic of Dublin keyhole escutcheons, the combination of arches in the stand is typical, and the lacquer decorations of the desk section, along with the flat details in the apron rails, are also determinative. Finally, its interior work, with its combination of pine and hardwoods in the drawer, the sides of which are joined by delicate wood shims, is also representative of a Dublin rather than a Dutch production.

The delicately balanced bureau de dame (45 and 48) has been authoritatively published[1] as made and labeled by one Hugh Granger, a seventeenth-century London seller of "household goods at reasonable rates," who apparently died prior to August 24, 1706. The irresolute *circa* date of 1710 given by such experts, (obviously not within Granger's lifetime) and a London origin are both quite impossible. Such a dainty masterpiece of highly skilled cabinetwork in choice walnut veneers, with highly sophisticated lacquer decorations, clearly can not have resulted from a training in seventeenth-century designs of cabinetmaking and lacquer techniques. With its superlative quality in those respects, and its principal surface a bevelled mirror plate that would have been an expensive item, especially in the London market, this elegant *tour de force* can hardly have been made to sell at a reasonable rate. Its highly individual design and decorative treatments are entirely characteristic, however, of work carried out *circa* 1730 or later, rather than around the turn of the seventeenth century, and in Dublin rather than London. Also, the exact leg, with its unusual terminal, is found in mahogany furniture, thus associating the entire composition with that period rather than with the oak and walnut years of Granger's lifespan.

As these are armchair opinions it is shown in confirmation that the interior of the slant-front bureau section is duplicated in its entirety by that of the typical Dublin dressing mirror (47), including the singularly scrolled drawer partitions, coved door, and flanking carved and fluted pilasters; the fanciful lacquer decorations are entirely characteristic of Dublin artistry (*cf* 46, 49 and *passim*); and the unusually shallow cornice conforms with that of the Irish secretaire (43), which is a very late piece with lever locks, *c.* 1790, rather than dating from the Queen Anne period to which it has been incorrectly assigned. While foreign to London techniques of design, similar insignificant pendants do mar the rails of various Georgian tables and stands, as in (44).

Half-tone illustrations in these proving files provide much further documentation. The entire upper section of this "labeled" piece is repeated in other Dublin secretaires of the same narrow width, shallow cornice and simply arched mirror door. One is veneered in Irish yew. Several are entirely surfaced with decorative lacquer work. In two lacquer examples the central section is fitted with a dressing drawer the front of which is shaped in a typical Dublin fashion of the time, varying from those illustrated here (35, 36, 38) but appearing in another Dublin dressing mirror (Elwood, 57) owned by Lady Wolseley. One of these lacquer secretaires illustrated in a Symonds magazine article has an underbody of three drawers and in typical Dublin fashion rests on four claw-and-ball feet.

With all of this evidence it can be accepted without any possible margin of error that the so-called Granger piece could not have been produced anywhere during the later seventeenth century as has been suggested, or around the time of his death. Instead it was produced two or more decades later, a differentiation often applicable between the dating by English experts, and the actual dates of unrecognized Dublin furniture and looking glasses illustrated as *English*. This is just one more instance of a fraudulently labeled piece, such as those that have passed through my own hands during the past fifty years; the piece itself is just as typical of Dublin in form and every detail as it is not characteristic of London in any respect.[2]

In its general design the walnut secretaire (43) was also made with the upper section surmounting a slant-front writing desk, and with lower drawers sliding within single, wide, half-round or astragal moldings. These examples are dated as *circa* 1700 by English experts, which is just as inexcusable as exhibiting the illustrated piece as of the Queen Anne period or even as in the Queen Anne style, for the cock-beaded, fall-front writing drawer precludes the use of either classification.

That piece may also serve to indicate why so many Dublin looking glasses of the middle or later eighteenth century appear with walnut frames, for thus it is obvious that a use of walnut continued in Dublin, as in Philadelphia, for many years after mahogany came into a wide popularity. Merely because a piece appears in walnut is no reason to assume that it belongs to the Walnut Period of English authorities. It should also be clear that classifications advanced by John Rogers and subsequently by R. W. Symonds in regard to the dating of Queen Anne and Georgian furniture according to the various types of moldings surrounding or planted on drawer facings, cannot be viewed as generally applicable.

As the leading authority on English, Irish and Continental furniture, Symonds published such palatial mirrors as (65-68) as "probably Continental," obviously without the knowledge that their eglomisé panels point only to Venice as the capital city of their derivation, had they not been produced in the Irish capital by Venetian craftsmen employed there. In fact some of the finest and most important carved and gilded pier mirrors in the whole of the British Isles were designed and executed, probably *en situ*, to conform with the interior architecture of such a palatial residence as Powerscourt, in County Wicklow, adjacent to County Dublin.

Gradual changes in the succeeding plainer frames eventually resulted in arched headings such as those of (69) and of (70), which seems indeed to have acquired an American character since its arrival in this country some two centuries ago.

Viscount Bateman's chest (71) is especially important in confirming the Dublin origin of pier mirrors and tables (*cf* 95, 96, 99 and 114) by means of its masks, shells, gadrooning and linked scrolls.

With eagles and eagle heads so much a part of Dublin furniture and mirror-frame designs, the card table (77) serves to show a favorite retrorse aspect in these heads, as in the following mirror frame and many others (*vide* also 108). In a special magazine article by R. W. Symonds ["A Red Lacquer Mirror," *The Connoisseur*, January 1930], such a Dublin pier glass is illustrated in color, with an entirely gilded cresting featuring a pair of such retrorsed eagle heads. It was correctly stated to be "distinctly a 'rara avis'"; a London counterpart would be rarer still.

A frame made for a Dublin silk-and-wool tapestry portait of King Geoge II, woven in 1738[3], provides one important clue in establishing the origin and approximate date of mirrors such as (86), (88), (90), and in linking them to the same school of carving responsible for such supposedly Charles II productions, as plate 87. Former authorities such as Herbert Cescinsky and R. W. Symonds completely ignored the tectonic methods employed in fashioning the drawers continued in such cabinets, which were not introduced prior to the middle and later Georgian years. Mirrors of a similar nature were brought to the attention of Symonds by a specialist in oak furniture. Always receptive to the prompting of certain dealers, he immediately gave them the desired publicity, eventually featuring one particular example in his most important opus, *English Furniture Making in the 17th and 18th Century* as "of the time of Charles II" (Fig. 198).

An especially determinative example of such carving appeared in a Scottish collection, displaying the royal British coat-of-arms rather than the usual cresting of cupids supporting an escutcheon, coronet or basket of flowers and wheat ears. This was said to have been "originally presented by King George II to the Earl of Hyndford." Dating from the later years of that monarch's rule (1727-1760), mahogany side tables have incorporated the same figural and foliage swags or festoons as those more common to the stands of lacquer cabinets (87 and 89).

The most characteristic features of Dublin pier tables are also the most obvious where either of two favorite methods have been employed in regard to their marble tops. One method appears in (95) and (99), where the marble slabs have been recessed within shallow edge moldings. In the other, an overhanging marble slab is fashioned with diagonally crossetted front corners, in combination with simple rear projections, as in (96) and (111). The slabs for such tables could be obtained from native formations of excellent marbles, as the mottled of Fermanagh, the green of Galway, and the black of Kilkenny.

Typical Dublin shells, running fret bands, regular and retrorsed volutes appear in the illustrations 105 to 111. The design of 109[4], recorded as made for the Duke of Devonshire, fits into a long sequence of such pier tables including those also made for Houghton Hall, Cassiobury Park and Longford Castle. A treatment favored in contemporary pier mirrors appears in the matt or sanded grounds of flat border surfaces (106, 113, etc.). Also, certain moldings appear in exactly the same combined groupings, for instance as in (110) and (113); in the former instance a sanded border may have been eliminated in the removal of gilding or paint.

Baskets of flowers, fruit and wheat ears—the *corbeilles* of European architecture—were favored by Dublin carvers and artists in gesso (49, 90, 91, 120, 168-170). The particular skill expended on the plaited basketry effect in plate 120 is representative of a technical proficiency that has resulted in so many of Dublin's furniture masterpieces being attributed to Vile and Cobb, or William Vile, as such modern-day exports from Ireland have increasingly arrived in the London market.

The maker of the architectural pier mirror, 125, John Teahan, Keeper, Art and Industrial Division, of the National Museum of Ireland, Dublin, has been able to locate as Joshua Kearney, carver and gilder, at 186 Great Britain Street, from 1795 to around 1805. He then moved to 49 Henry Street, where he remained until at least 1820.

A group of Dublin secretaires that have been mistakenly ascribed to German origins are fitted with mirrored doors in flat-arched headings following the lines of those in 130. A related group of Dublin pier glasses with similarly arched mirror panels has served in disproving those ascriptions. Their frames will feature pilasters with richly carved capitals (135 and 136), while some appear with a carved satyr mask at the base or superimposed on a latticed frieze. The secretaire (130) shows that particular flat-arched shaping, with also a characteristic pediment and bird finial. Additionally, it is important toward the identification of Dublin furniture with matching brass fittings and similar coved stellate inlays.

The entirely representative Dublin looking glass (132) is exhibited as an "English" production in the "Dutch Style," this without the most elementary knowledge of designs in either field. Here again is a complete disregard of Dublin's presence as one of the greatest capital city furniture-producing centers in all Europe, far greater in importance than the capital of Holland and all of her subsidiary production centers combined.

That disregard is vividly emphasized when another such Dublin example (142) is exhibited in the same museum, not again as English, but as American. A corresponding example (143) was contained in a collection of British furniture auctioned in New York City with no thought of considering it as other than English, certainly not as American, or at least not until time might permit its appearance in a sale of Old English Furniture to have been forgotten.

With these varying acceptances of such Dublin parcel-gilded walnut or mahogany looking glasses, it has been considered as possibly useful, particularly to collectors of Americana, to utilize Plate 116 as a divider separating those examples more generally distributed throughout the British Isles, from designs of those exported to America or frequently accepted as originating here.

Dublin's productivity in the manufacture of looking glasses for distribution throughout the British Isles and to America is especially evident in the number and diversity of its Chippendale carved and gilded wall mirrors remaining today. The more simplified of these often complex compositions have been singled out by museum authorities here as the work of American manufactories that simply did not exist. One of the more elementary of such Chippendale examples has been published in *Antiques* magazine as owned by Samuel Harris Gardiner and "Made for Richard Edwards by John Elliott of Philadelphia." In this instance at long last there is a Chippendale carved and gilded looking glass, *sold* by John Elliott, in regard to which it can be stated with absolute certainty that it was obtained from Dublin. Although not as fine in design or carving as the examples selected for illustration here, it was no doubt supplied by one of the lesser manufactories of that capital city. Even to the parallel hatchings of the frills on its C-scrolls (as in the top edging of 194), and similar markings in the leaves and blossoms of its side pendants, all of the carving is typical of these exportations to Great Britain and America. Possibly through some resemblances to that particular frame, accepted here as stocked by Elliott along with his more general household supplies, another such Chippendale example of only fair quality, in the Metropolitan Museum, has also been mistakenly designated as "American, 18th Century, Philadelphia Chippendale style."

The importance of minute details in comparative studies of antique furniture may be illustrated at this point in the trifoliate capitals, with incurvate bifurcate headings, of the

The Development of Dublin Looking Glasses

slender lateral piers featured in (214, 215, 216 and 226). These examples and dozens of others represented in file photographs and halftones, all arranged systematically in gradually developing sequences of designs, make it immediately apparent that (along with its other Dublin furnishings) two pairs of magnificent mirrors at Crichel, in Dorset, published as "Probably by Thomas Chippendale,"[5] were also obtained from the Irish capital. Similarly, two pairs of equally important Chippendale wall mirrors were included among the Dublin furnishings of Bramshill, in Hampshire; these are credited as "probably by Linnell" (vide *Dictionary of English Furniture*, Fig. 63-64).

From these discoveries it has also been possible to ascertain the acquisition of Dublin Chippendale looking glasses by Lord Leigh for Stonleigh Abbey, and by Viscount Cobham for Hagley Hall. For St. Giles House, near Crichel in Dorset, the Earl of Shaftesbury also obtained matching pier tables as well as mirrors from Dublin, in preference to any that might have been available in London.

Early in these researches it had been clear that British residences in western counties, located along the Bristol and St. George's Channels and northward along the Irish Sea, would in preference have ordered their more important furniture from nearby Dublin rather than far-off London. When it was found that this had indeed been the case in regard to Badminton House, in Gloucestershire, that supposition was reinforced and still further studies were concentrated on the furniture of collections located along those shores.

Eventually it was noticed, however, that other important, originally formed British collections containing Dublin furniture and looking glasses, Waterford chandelieres, etc., were situated additionally in southern maritime counties and, increasingly it was found, in inland counties more closely encircling London. Then it was finally realized that although residences such as Badminton might be located in those western counties of first interest, nevertheless others might also be situated within a hundred miles of London, and still their original owners had favored Dublin furnishings over those of the English capital.

Superficial attitudes toward accuracy in research are obvious in the suppositions advanced by those experts of the museum exhibiting both the Badminton House bed (219) and the mirror (220) *en suite* not only with its design, but also with that of the Badminton House mirror illustrated by Percy Macquoid (*Age of Satinwood*, Fig. 8), and with that of (221) here. The bed until just recently has been claimed by various experts as the work of Thomas Chippendale, but of late the Linnels have been speculated on as capable of designing and producing such a masterpiece. None of these experts has considered its dragon finials as especially distinctive or of any particular value toward affirming or negating their attributions; and none can have noticed any identifying significance in the fact that the same hand is indicated as also responsible for those of the wall mirror (220) that, with an equal lack of any evidence whatsoever, has for years been exhibited as *German!*

Some of the furniture at Badminton House has been described as in the 'Director' style though having no real dependence on that publication. According to Edwards & Jourdain[6]

> The famous Chinese bedroom there is described by Dr. Pocoke (*Travels Through England*, Vol. 2, p. 31) in 1754 as "finished and furnished very elegantly in the Chinese manner," which affords evidence of the date. The room, which is hung with Chinese wallpaper, contained japanned furniture and a bedstead, japanned black with gilt details, which is "one of the most successful examples of the Chinese vogue" (Oliver Brackett, *Thomas Chippendale*, p. 186). It has some affinities with a design for a bed with a

pagoda-shaped canopy in the *Director* (Plate XXXII). The pagoda-shaped roof is surmounted by a vase with acanthus foliage in gilt metal; and at each corner is an upward-curved scroll bearing a dragon in carved and gilt wood. The back is filled with "Chinese paling," and this filling was also used for the back and arms of chairs . . . All these pieces are of conspicuously high quality, and while there is no definite evidence, the Duke's subscription to the *Director* and the date of the group would seem to point to Chippendale's responsibility.[!!]

The fact that Dr. Pocock's description of the Duke of Beaufort's famous Chinese bedroom was published in 1754, while Chippendale's *Director* was not issued in London until that year, should give pause for thought and careful reasoning. The designing and manufacture of that bedstead, as ordered and delivered from Dublin, could hardly have been influenced by Chippendale in London. Along with the designs he had drawn upon or copied outright for his *Director*, could it not in fact be that he was also conversant with those already offered in Dublin?

The year 1754 is of exceptional interest in determining the stage of development that had already been reached by that time in Dublin's handling of Chinese-Chippendale themes. As one of the very few instances in which a definite calculation of time may thus be applied to related masterpieces, this recording also compensates for the unwillingness of the present duke to divulge any information regarding the furniture masterpieces ordered prior to or after that date by his progenitor.

Proof is also provided that while Dublin furniture styles were frequently developed or retained later than related effects in London, this was not the case with Dublin's ascendancy in the production of such Chippendale masterpieces, acknowledged by leading English authorities of such high quality as to point to Chippendale's responsibility—with his shop thus considered as the only one in London capable of such work!

In contrast to the degree of sophistication reached by or just prior to 1754 in these particular Dublin designs, it should be remembered that earlier themes were followed simultaneously in the continued popularity of earlier Georgian forms such as those featured in seat furniture with solid or interlaced splats and cabriole legs terminating in pad, paw, or claw-and-ball feet.

The unusually large looking glass made for Tyrone House, in Dublin (222), an especially obvious Dublin extravaganza, has been entirely unrecognizable to the foremost authority on old Irish residences. It is attributed to Thomas Johnson[7] in its publication and thus presented as a London example; by the president of the Irish Georgian Society who has thus shown the same lack of interest and comprehension that has become prevalent throughout Ireland today, where admittedly no criteria are recognized through which to distinguish between Irish and English furniture, and thus no attention has been paid to Dublin as a manufacturing center of such masterpieces—the only world capital to suffer such disregard.

It has become apparent during these researches that London also did not attempt to compete with Dublin in the later Hepplewhite, Sheraton and Regency looking glasses that specially featured gesso or carton pierre ornamentation. The same is true in regard to Dublin's resurgence in the use of eglomisé decorations. In these there are often riverside scenes that the unobservant may associate with various English localities, or that in

America are invariably designated as Hudson River views or other native waterways, but that generally tend to reinforce attributions of New York origins. In reality they depict rural effects with rustic fences and bridges, windmills, castles, and plaster-walled cottages with palm-thatched roofs, all crying for recognition as typical of Irish country landscapes (*vide* 192, 272, 274).

Examples matching the Regency overmantel (280) have been published by experts on Americana under such dates as 1781-83, as identifiable with Samuel McIntyre of Salem, Massachusetts, and even as having been "made in Paris, France, in 1801." The one shown here is not the much publicized example from the Pierce Nichols house in Salem, but is from the Wadsworth family of that same town.

The ribbed candle cups and trays of (250, 282 and 285) are representative of Dublin metalwork during this general period; along with those of (295) they are quite as distinctive as the Waterford or other glass fittings represented in plates (283) and (287).

Because of the great amount of Dublin furniture and looking glasses that have been so persistently published as Dutch, though having no connection whatsoever with the designs and working techniques of that country, a pier mirror entirely characteristic of that country has been included here (300) as a single ray of enlightenment in this great waste of published material.

The sunburst or sunray frame, fitted with a clock as in (301) or with a looking glass, is also frequently designated as Dutch, though sometimes as French. From those examples appearing in illustrations of old Irish residences, and the popularity of such motifs in Dublin seat furniture and cabinetwork, there may be special reasons for the divergence of opinions. As an echo of an old-time dealer's remark that "Irish furniture was not popular so we called everything English," in such instances "Dutch" may have been substituted here, since no comparable English examples exist; or, with the ever increasing values of French furniture, additional profit may have been sought in that field of interest.

---

1. Edwards & Jourdain, *Georgian Cabinet-Makers* (London, 1955), 210, 211. Also published, with label, by R. W. Symonds.
2. The stand of this distinctive Dublin *tour de force* matches an inlaid walnut tray-top table, lot 1674 in The Benjamin Sonnenberg Collection, sold in June, 1979, as "DUTCH circa 1720."
3. Vide *The Connoisseur*, September, 1959.
4. The marble slab is not crossetted in conformity with the typical Dublin frieze treatment, and is apparently not original.
5. Edwards & Jourdain, *Georgian Cabinet-Makers* (London, 1955), 120, 121.
6. *Georgian Cabinet-Makers* (London, 1955), pp. 70-71.
7. Desmond Guiness & William Ryan, *Irish Houses & Castles*, (London, 1971).

Distributors of Colonial and Early Federal Looking Glasses

DESPITE THE RELIANCE of American colonists on importations of window glasses, looking glasses, coach and chariot glasses, table glasses and glass lighting fixtures, the mirrors sold at "wholesale and retail" by John Elliott and his son, of Philadelphia, and those distributed by William Wilmerding, Stephen Whiting, James Stokes, Wayne and Biddle, etc., are still largely believed to have been manufactured here. Otherwise it is generally assumed that they were imported from England in the usual countrywide speculation, with no possibility of a capital city specification. Illustrations of such mirrors in walnut or mahogany frames and others closely resembling them in designs or decorative features have been set apart in separate files throughout the many years of these researches, on the off chance that they might indeed have had closer ties to London than merely being on shipboard at that point for homeward bound vessels, a circumstantial detail constantly belabored in Elliott advertisements:

1762: John Elliott "Imported in the Polly, Capt. Wynn, and other Ships late from London . . ."
1762: John Elliott "has imported in the Philadelphia Packet, Capt. Badden and other ships from London . . . Looking Glasses, consisting of Chimney Glasses, Pier and Sconce Glasses of most sizes and fashions, Dressing Glasses, Shaving Glasses, painted, fram'd and Pocket Glasses . . ."
1763: John Elliott "Imported in the Hanover Packet, Capt. Falconer, and other vessels from London . . ."
1768: John Elliott "Imported in the Mary and Elizabeth, Capt. Sparks; and other vessels from London, and to be sold wholesale and retail . . . A very large and neat and general assortment of looking glasses and a large assortment of coach and chariot glasses. . . ."

There was no city in all of England, other than London, with capacities equal to meeting American demands for looking glasses. However, with these and other related needs obtainable in only one or the other of the two British metropolitan centers, tax conscious Americans would not have submitted to the inordinate assessments in addition to the costs of such productions in the high priced London market, when all such necessities and luxuries could be obtained at one cost, tax-free, in Dublin. Additionally, mirrors of the types handled by the Elliotts, Wilmerding, etc. cannot on any basis of fact be seriously attributed to designing and manufacture in London.

Only after all other problems had been cleared up were those mirror designs relating to the Elliotts and Wilmerding finally approached. Although by then, with the present volume completed to this point, it appeared as a foregone conclusion that their mirrors had been obtained in the only reasonably acceptable market to which so many closely related examples had been traced, the possibility of such relationships not being absolute demanded further direct and conclusive proofs.

There was reason for exercising special caution because of early claims by the senior Elliott that he had for sale "all sorts of English Looking-glasses at the lowest Rates." Whether this had been prompted primarily through misrepresentation on the part of a possible middleman, or merely through a liberty taken in a broad acceptance of "English" as applying to the British Isles as a whole, the claim was dropped in his later advertisements and in those of his son. Only through a recent, separate study of Elliott-labeled mirrors, their distinctive bird finial (313), and other frames on which it has appeared, together with still further considerations, was that statement of Elliott's finally and conclusively proved as incorrect and misleading. Now it may be said that the period over which Dublin manufactures have been successfully concealed from the public dates from Elliott's time at least, rather than just since the collecting of antique furniture and looking glasses came into vogue during the latter half of the nineteenth century.

According to American nomenclature, mirrors such as (306, 307 and 308) are termed as "Queen Anne" in style. As a recent arrival here, (309) has been judged to date between 1727 and 1760 by its British designation of "George II," though *circa* 1760 would be more precise.

An easily overlooked feature of (310), repeated in the Elliott-labeled example (313), is that the inside molding or plate surround is curved and cusped at all four corners. This contrasts with the usual compositions in which lower corners are generally squared. Along with (311 and 316), these are the only frames with this seldom carried out treatment to appear in the entirety of my files.

The Elliott-labeled mirror (313) was sold for only $450 against an auction value of only $400; while a similar example in the Reifsnyder Sale (659) dated 1753-1760, brought $4,200. Another typical Dublin pier glass of a handsome architectural design approximating that of (141) brought $3,100 in a Philadelphia auction sale of May 14th, 1930. As a "Constitution mirror" this was accredited to manufacture in "Philadelphia, *circa* 1760," with attention drawn to a label fragment suggested as possibly that of Elliott.

American importers of Dublin trade mirrors were not the only ones affixing their own store labels to the backboards. For instance, at the time that mirrors with eglomisé panels such as shown in (269) were being imported and labeled by James Stokes, other Dublin examples on the order of those from (276 to 279) were being labeled by "J. N. O. Marnoch, Carver and Gilder, No. 12 Princess Street, Edinburgh."

James Stokes was succeeded by Wayne and Biddle at Market and Front Streets in Philadelphia. In their general store as well as in that of John Elliott, dressing mirrors similar to (41) but with ogee-molded and -scrolled bracket feet as in (55, 57 and 61) were also handled; in both instances they have been found with store labels still intact.

A most recent private contribution to these researches is indeed worthy of inclusion here, especially to emphasize the most important reasons for Dublin's commercial ascendancy over London in her wide distribution of looking glasses to America and throughout the British Isles. The Chippendale pier mirror with eagle console plate 224 is representative of a pair that was designed and executed for an important residence in Shropshire, which like many others in neighboring English and Welsh counties as far as transportation was concerned, was much more conveniently situated in respect to Dublin than to London. Additionally, an extra deterrent would have been the exorbitant excise taxes to be levied on the mirror plates had somewhat similar pieces been ordered from London; as those same taxes, both before and after the Revolution, had been so continuously avoided by the American colonists.

Addendum

ADDITIONAL CHARACTERISTIC EXAMPLES of Dublin looking glasses from *The Collection of Norman Adams*, are illustrated in a recent book (1983) by Stevens and Whittington, boldly entitled *18th Century English Furniture*, in which there is a much larger presentation of Dublin seat furniture and cabinetwork. English of course is the long overworked misnomer for those capital-city masterpieces of Queen Anne and Georgian furniture that cannot be accurately claimed as having been made in London. That designation and the customary chitchat about London craftsmen and designers would have been ignored also in this instance except for one incorrect statement about a Dublin maker's label affixed to a Regency sofa or writing table, p. 168, that of Mack, Williams and Gibton.

This Dublin firm achieved such high recognition in London that it was privileged to advertise itself as *Cabinet Makers to His Majesty*; the only such honor noted by Edwards and Jourdain in the entirety of their work on *Georgian Cabinet-Makers*. There they are recorded as *Upholsterers and Cabinet Makers to His Majesty, His Excellency the Lord Lieutenant and the Rt. Hon. His Majesty's Board of Works, 39 Stratford (for Stafford) Street, Dublin*.

Stevens and Whittington have incorrectly stated the wording of the label on that Norman Adams table by eliminating the entire reference to *Mack, Williams and Gibton* as being *Cabinet Makers to His Majesty*; and by referring to that august firm of Dublin cabinet-makers as *Upholders* (sic) *to the Rt. Honble* (sic) *and Honble* (sic) *His Majesty's Board of Works*.

Incidentally, Norman Adams was one of the contributors to my *Directory of the Historic Cabinet Woods*, back in 1953. It had been obvious from his magazine advertisements that he was obtaining his Queen Anne and Georgian furniture from the then ever increasing supplies of the Dublin antique market. When it became noticeable that photographs I requested of the more distinctively treated Dublin importations were Not Available to me, I returned all of his photographs of the plainer examples.

In mentioning Mack, Williams and Gibton, Edwards and Jourdain specified that *Each of a pair of fine serpentine-fronted mahogany commodes, c. 1760, with elaborate brass rococo handles, formerly in the Samuel Courtauld Collection, bears the label of these makers.* As the firm did not exist c. 1760, and that partnership continued only from 1815 to 1825, those two commodes are of especial importance to all serious researchists in, and collectors of, fine and superfine Late Chippendale furniture; as continuously developed in Dublin during the latest Georgian years and the earlier part of the Victorian era.

It is therefore earnestly hoped that the present whereabouts of one or both of those documentary Chippendale commodes will soon be disclosed, and that a photograph may be obtained to show their design, and the rococo pattern of their equally important Late Chippendale handles.

My greatest hope is to be able to see, and if possible to publish a photo of one of the M.,W.&G. commodes with their documentary handles.

Plates

PLATE 1

1 "CAROLEAN" WALNUT ARMORIAL LOOKING GLASS

PLATE 2

2 "CAROLEAN" TORTOISESHELL AND EBONY ARMORIAL LOOKING GLASS

3 "CAROLEAN" FRET-CARVED WALNUT LOOKING GLASS

PLATE 3

4 "CAROLEAN" FRET-CARVED WALNUT LOOKING GLASS

PLATE 4

5 "CAROLEAN" WALNUT MARQUETRY LOOKING GLASS

6 "CAROLEAN" WALNUT MARQUETRY LOOKING GLASS. Victoria & Albert Museum. Crown Copyright.

PLATE 6

7 "CAROLEAN" MARQUETRY FALL-FRONT WRITING CABINET. With original Dublin handles and escutcheons. Exhibited as *Dutch. Late XVII Century*. Victoria & Albert Museum. Crown Copyright.

PLATE 7

8   QUEEN ANNE PARCEL-GILDED WALNUT PIER MIRROR

9   QUEEN ANNE PARCEL-GILDED WALNUT "AMERICAN" PIER MIRROR

PLATE 8

10 CHIPPENDALE CARVED AND GILDED WALL MIRROR

11 QUEEN ANNE WALNUT PIER MIRROR

12 QUEEN ANNE WALNUT PIER MIRROR

PLATE 10

13   QUEEN ANNE WALNUT PIER MIRROR

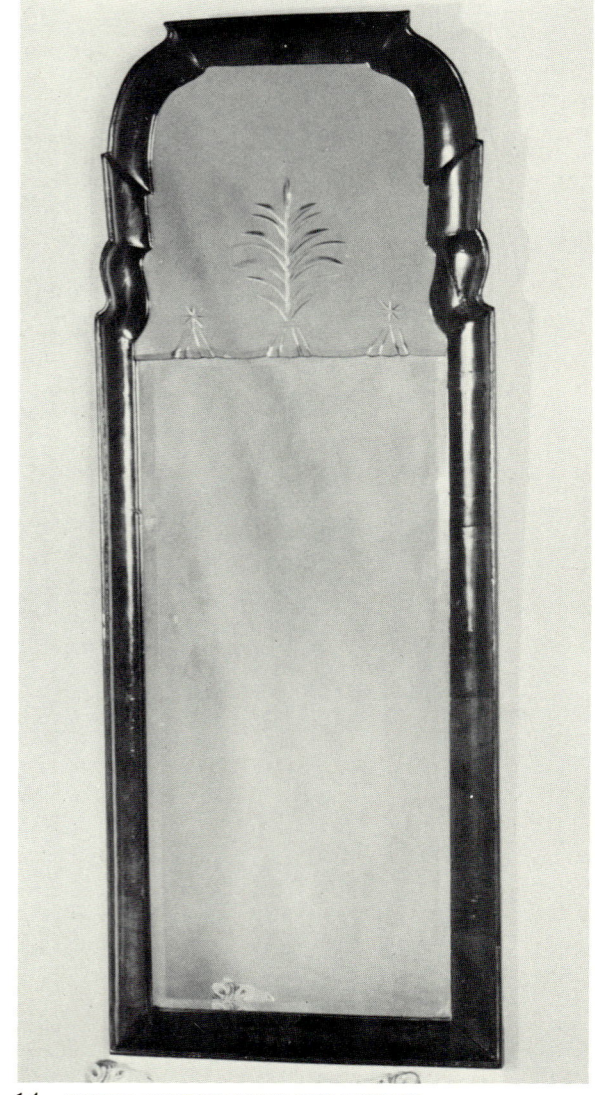

14   QUEEN ANNE WALNUT PIER MIRROR

PLATE 11

16 UPPER SECTION, QUEEN ANNE FRET-CARVED AND DECORATED LACQUER PIER MIRROR. Exhibited as *American XVIII Century, probably from Massachusetts.* Metropolitan Museum of Art.

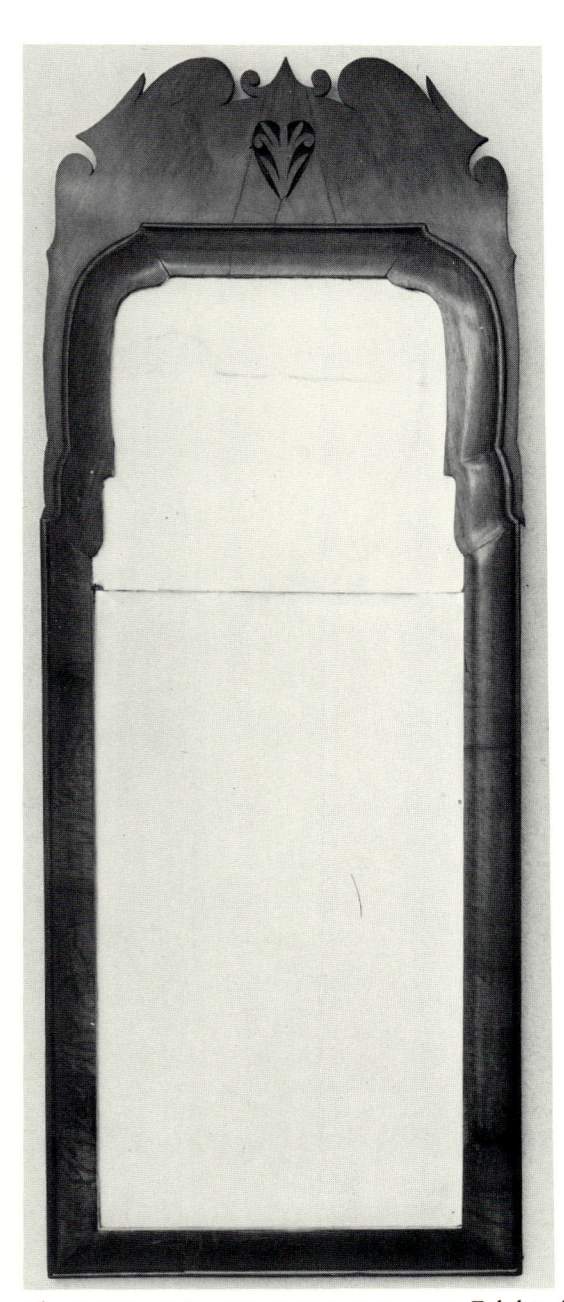

15 QUEEN ANNE MAHOGANY PIER MIRROR. Exhibited as *American 1700-1725.* Metropolitan Museum of Art.

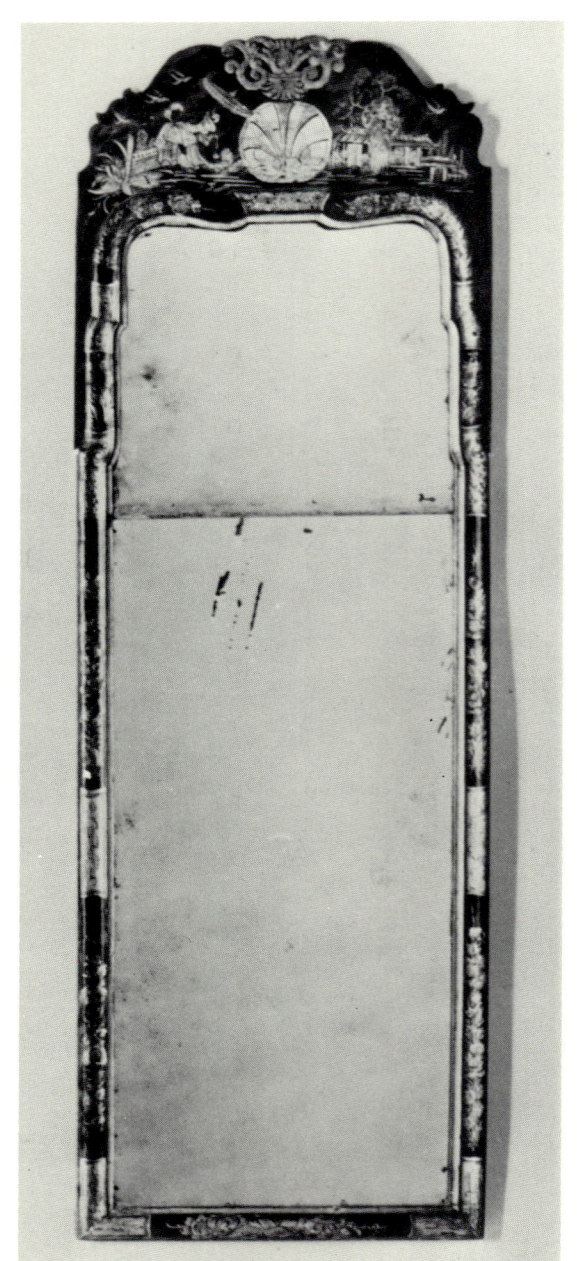

PLATE 12

17 QUEEN ANNE DECORATED LACQUER PIER MIRROR.
Exhibited as *American XVIII Century, Boston, Mass.*, ca.
1735. Metropolitan Museum of Art.

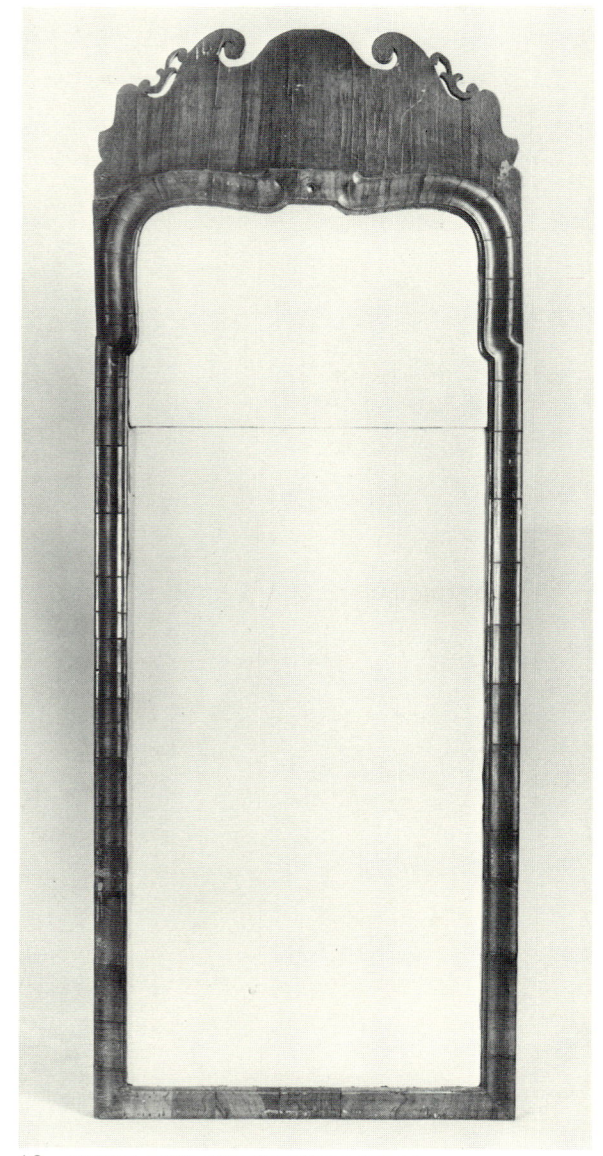

18 QUEEN ANNE WALNUT PIER MIRROR

PLATE 13

19-20-21   EARLY GEORGIAN DECORATED LACQUER PIER MIRROR AND PAIR OF GIRANDOLES. Exhibited as *American or English*.

PLATE 14

22 LATE GEORGIAN DECORATED LACQUER CORNER CABINET. *Cf* lacquer work with that of 19, 20, 21 and 23-25. Metropolitan Museum of Art.

23 GEORGIAN DECORATED LACQUER SECRETAIRE. Exhibited as *English or Dutch*.

PLATE 16

24 LATE GEORGIAN DECORATED LACQUER CABINET ON CARVED AND GILDED STAND. Produced about a century later than the reign of Charles II.

PLATE 17

25 EARLY GEORGIAN DECORATED LACQUER PIER MIRROR. Exhibited as *English (probably)* ca. *1725*. Metropolitan Museum of Art.

26 EARLY GEORGIAN WALNUT PIER MIRROR

PLATE 18

27 CHIPPENDALE PARCEL-GILDED WALNUT "PHILADELPHIA" MIRROR

28 CHIPPENDALE PARCEL-GILDED WALNUT PIER MIRROR. Metropolitan Museum of Art.

PLATE 19

29 CHIPPENDALE PARCEL-GILDED WALNUT PIER MIRROR. Sold as American.

PLATE 20

30 CHIPPENDALE PARCEL-GILDED WALNUT LOOKING GLASS. Sold as American or English.

31 CHIPPENDALE PARCEL-GILDED WALNUT "PHILADELPHIA" MIRROR

32 CHIPPENDALE PARCEL-GILDED WALNUT "PHILADELPHIA" PIER MIRROR

PLATE 22

33 CHIPPENDALE PARCEL-GILDED WALNUT "ENGLISH" PIER MIRROR

34 CHIPPENDALE PARCEL-GILDED WALNUT "AMERICAN" PIER MIRROR.

PLATE 23

35 QUEEN ANNE DECORATED LACQUER DRESSING MIRROR

PLATE 24

36 QUEEN ANNE DECORATED LACQUER "DUTCH" BUREAU-DRESSING TABLE

PLATE 25

37 EARLY GEORGIAN DECORATED LACQUER DRESSING MIRROR. Victoria & Albert Museum. Crown Copyright.

PLATE 26

38 EARLY GEORGIAN DECORATED LACQUER DRESSING MIRROR

39 EARLY GEORGIAN DECORATED LACQUER DRESSING MIRROR. Exhibited as *American XVII Century; ca 1720*. Metropolitan Museum of Art.

40 GEORGIAN WALNUT DRESSING MIRROR

41 GEORGIAN WALNUT DRESSING MIRROR. A similar example in mahogany labeled by John Elliott of Philadelphia.

PLATE 27

42 EARLY GEORGIAN CARVED AND INLAID WALNUT BUREAU WITH DRESSING MIRROR

PLATE 28

43 LATE GEORGIAN WALNUT SECRETAIRE. Exhibited as of the "Queen Anne period, English XVIII Century." Metropolitan Museum of Art.

44 GEORGIAN CARVED MAHOGANY TRAY-TOP TABLE. *Cf* insignificant frieze pendant with that of 45.

PLATE 29

45 GEORGE II WALNUT AND DECORATED LACQUER DRESSING BUREAU. Courtesy of Christie, Manson & Woods, London.

PLATE 30

46 EARLY GEORGIAN DECORATED LACQUER DRESSING MIRROR. Victoria & Albert Museum. Crown Copyright.

47 GEORGE II INLAID WALNUT DRESSING MIRROR. *Cf* interior of desk section with that of 48.

PLATE 31

48 GEORGE II DRESSING BUREAU. Open view of 45. Courtesy of Christie, Manson & Woods, London.

PLATE 32

49 LATE GEORGIAN DECORATED LACQUER CABINET WITH CARVED AND GILDED CRESTING. Victoria & Albert Museum. Crown Copyright.

PLATE 33

50 CHIPPENDALE CARVED MAHOGANY DRESSING MIRROR
51 CHIPPENDALE CARVED MAHOGANY ARCHITECTURAL COMMODE. The handles of a very favorite Dublin pattern.

PLATE 34

52 CHIPPENDALE CARVED AND GILDED DRESSING MIRROR

53 CHIPPENDALE FRET-CARVED MAHOGANY WALL MIRROR

PLATE 35

54 LATE CHIPPENDALE MAHOGANY DRESSING MIRROR.
Metropolitan Museum of Art.

55 HEPPLEWHITE FRET-CARVED MAHOGANY DRESSING MIRROR

61

PLATE 36

56 HEPPLEWHITE INLAID MAHOGANY DRESSING MIRROR

57 HEPPLEWHITE INLAID MAHOGANY DRESSING MIRROR

58-59 LATE GEORGIAN INLAID MAHOGANY DRESSING MIRRORS
60 LATE GEORGIAN INLAID MAHOGANY TWO-PILLAR SOFA TABLE. A key two-pillar form eventually leading to the discovery of Dublin's supremacy in the designing and manufacture of sofa tables.

61 HEPPLEWHITE INLAID MAHOGANY DRESSING MIRROR
62 HEPPLEWHITE MAHOGANY BOW-FRONT CHEST OF DRAWERS

PLATE 38

63 GEORGE III MAHOGANY BASIN STAND WITH SHAVING MIRROR

64 GEORGE III INLAID AND DECORATED CHEVAL GLASS.
Victoria & Albert Museum. Crown Copyright.

PLATE 39

65 QUEEN ANNE GILDED PIER MIRROR WITH VENETIAN-TYPE EGLOMISÉ BORDER. Victoria & Albert Museum. Crown Copyright.

PLATE 40

67 EXPERT RESTORATION OF CREST PANEL

66 QUEEN ANNE PIER MIRROR WITH EGLOMISÉ BORDER AND CRESTING. Courtesy of Mallett & Son (Antiques) Ltd., London.

PLATE 41

68 QUEEN ANNE GILDED OVERMANTEL WITH EGLOMISÉ BORDER, AND OIL PAINTING. Courtesy of Mallett & Son (Antiques) Ltd., London.

PLATE 42

69 QUEEN ANNE GILDED PIER GLASS WITH MIRROR BORDER

PLATE 43

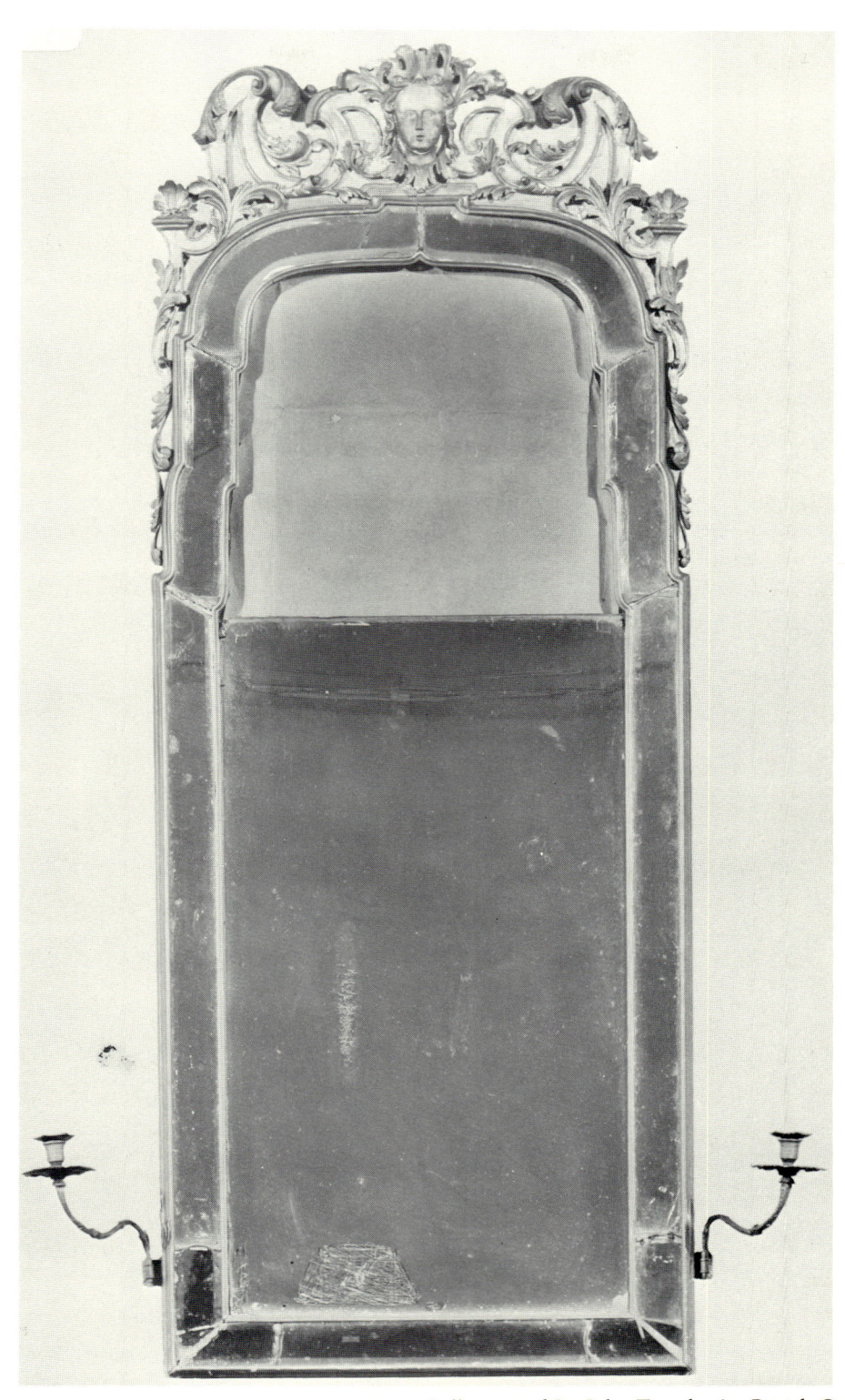

70 QUEEN ANNE GILDED PIER GLASS WITH MIRROR BORDER. Collection of Sir John Temple, 1st British Consul-General to the United States. Descended in the Temple-Winthrop-Minot Family of New York.

PLATE 44

71 EARLY GEORGIAN CARVED AND GILDED WOOD AND GESSO CHEST. With monogram of Viscount Bateman. Victoria & Albert Museum. Crown Copyright.

PLATE 45

72   EARLY GEORGIAN CARVED AND GILDED GIRANDOLE MIRROR. Courtesy of Charles Lumb & Sons Ltd., Harrogate.

PLATE 46

73 EARLY GEORGIAN GILDED PIER MIRROR WITH EGLOMISÉ BORDER AND CREST PANEL. Courtesy of Mallett & Son (Antiques) Ltd., London.

PLATE 47

74 EARLY GEORGIAN GILDED PIER GLASS WITH MIRROR BORDER. The urn finial, and crown cutting, also favored in Dublin secretaires.

PLATE 48

75 QUEEN ANNE PARCEL-GILDED WALNUT PIER MIRROR

PLATE 49

76   EARLY GEORGIAN GILDED GESSO WALL MIRROR. Courtesy of Charles Lumb & Sons Ltd., Harrogate.

PLATE 50

77 CHIPPENDALE MAHOGANY EAGLE-HEAD CARD TABLE. The eagle-head theme also of Dublin pier tables, 109, seat furniture, 134, and looking glasses: 78, 85, 108, 113, 114, 144, 161, 180. Metropolitan Museum of Art.

78 EARLY GEORGIAN GILDED GESSO WALL MIRROR. Courtesy of Charles Lumb & Sons Ltd., Harrogate.

PLATE 52

79 EARLY GEORGIAN GILDED GESSO WALL MIRROR. Courtesy of Charles Lumb & Sons Ltd., Harrogate.

80 EARLY GEORGIAN GILDED GESSO WALL MIRROR. Courtesy of Charles Lumb & Sons Ltd., Harrogate.

PLATE 54

81 EARLY GEORGIAN GILDED GESSO WALL MIRROR. Courtesy of Needham's Antiques, Inc., New York City.

82 EARLY GEORGIAN GILDED GESSO WALL MIRROR. Courtesy of Biggs of Maidenhead.

PLATE 56

83 EARLY GEORGIAN GILDED GESSO WALL MIRROR

84 EARLY GEORGIAN GILDED GESSO WALL MIRROR. Courtesy of J. J. Wolff (Antiques) Ltd., New York City.

PLATE 58

85   EARLY GEORGIAN GILDED GESSO WALL MIRROR. Courtesy of Needham's Antiques, Inc., New York City.

PLATE 59

86 GEORGE II GILDED WALL MIRROR WITH LAMP BRACKET. Courtesy of Asprey & Company Limited, London.

PLATE 60

87   LATE GEORGIAN DECORATED LACQUER CABINET ON CARVED AND GILDED STAND

PLATE 61

88 EARLY GEORGIAN GILDED CHERUB-HEAD FRAME. Courtesy of Asprey & Company Limited, London.

PLATE 62

89 LATE GEORGIAN DECORATED LACQUER CABINET. The stand carved with winged cherub heads, eagle, etc. Exhibited as *Charles II*. Victoria & Albert Museum. Crown Copyright.

PLATE 63

90 EARLY GEORGIAN GILDED OVAL WALL MIRROR. Carved with winged cherub head and favorite Dublin finial basket of flowers and fruit. Courtesy of Jeremy Ltd., London.

PLATE 64

91 EARLY GEORGIAN CARVED, PAINTED AND PARCEL-GILDED PIER TABLE

PLATE 65

92 EARLY GEORGIAN GILDED WALL MIRROR. With winged cherub head.

PLATE 66

93 EARLY GEORGIAN GILDED WALL MIRROR. With satyr and eagle heads.

PLATE 67

94 EARLY GEORGIAN GILDED PIER MIRROR. With an especial abundance of documentary features, the least being lateral cord-and-tassel pendants as also favored in Dublin seat furniture and cabinetwork. Exhibited as *English*, circa *1720*. Metropolitan Museum of Art.

PLATE 68

95 EARLY GEORGIAN GILDED PIER TABLE. The top slab inset as in 99. Cf carving with that of 96 and 98.

PLATE 69

96 EARLY GEORGIAN GILDED PIER TABLE. The slab distinctively shaped. The elaborated framework reflecting Continental influence. Victoria & Albert Museum. Crown Copyright.

PLATE 70

97 EARLY GEORGIAN PARCEL-GILDED WALNUT ARCHITECTURAL PIER MIRROR

98 EARLY GEORGIAN GILDED WALL MIRROR. Courtesy of J. J. Wolff (Antiques) Ltd., New York City.

PLATE 72

99 EARLY GEORGIAN CARVED AND GILDED PIER TABLE. The inset slab inlaid with specimen marbles. *Vide* 302. Courtesy of Mallett & Son (Antiques) Ltd., London.

PLATE 73

100 CHIPPENDALE CARVED AND GILDED WALL MIRROR. Courtesy of French & Co., Inc., New York City.

PLATE 74

101 EARLY GEORGIAN CARVED MAHOGANY PIER TABLE. The typical Dublin rococo shell- and leaf-carving repeated on matching architectural pier mirror.

102 CHIPPENDALE GILDED WALL MIRROR. With familiar spilling urns.

PLATE 76

103 EARLY GEORGIAN GILDED ARCHITECTURAL PIER MIRROR. Courtesy of Needham's Antiques, Inc., New York City.

PLATE 77

104 EARLY GEORGIAN GILDED ARCHITECTURAL PIER MIRROR. Courtesy of Needham's Antiques, Inc. New York City.

PLATE 78

105 EARLY GEORGIAN CARVED AND PARCEL-GILDED MAHOGANY PIER TABLE. With exceptionally distinctive ornamental treatments that also appear characteristically in Dublin mirror frames and, in smaller scale, on the aprons and legs of seat furniture. Victoria & Albert Museum. Crown Copyright.

PLATE 79

106   EARLY GEORGIAN GILDED ARCHITECTURAL PIER MIRROR. Victoria & Albert Museum. Crown Copyright.

PLATE 80

107 EARLY GEORGIAN CARVED MAHOGANY PIER TABLE. Victoria & Albert Museum. Crown Copyright.

PLATE 81

108 EARLY GEORGIAN CARVED PINE OVERMANTEL

PLATE 82

109 EARLY GEORGIAN CARVED AND GILDED PIER TABLE. Victoria & Albert Museum. Crown Copyright.

108

110   EARLY GEORGIAN CARVED PINE ARCHITECTURAL PIER MIRROR

PLATE 84

111   EARLY GEORGIAN CARVED AND GILDED PIER TABLE. C*f* shell finial of 131.

PLATE 85

112 EARLY GEORGIAN CARVED AND GILDED ARCHITECTURAL PIER MIRROR

PLATE 86

113 EARLY GEORGIAN GILDED FRAME WITH THERMOMETER, BAROMETER AND LAMP BRACKET. Victoria & Albert Museum. Crown Copyright.

PLATE 87

114 EARLY GEORGIAN GILDED ARCHITECTURAL PIER MIRROR WITH BOWES COAT-OF-ARMS. Exhibited as *English*, circa 1720. From Streatlan Castle, Durham, England. Metropolitan Museum of Art.

PLATE 88

115 EARLY GEORGIAN CARVED AND INLAID WALNUT CARD TABLE. The frieze centering a typical asymetrical shell carving.

PLATE 89

116 EARLY GEORGIAN CARVED PINE ARCHITECTURAL PIER MIRROR

PLATE 90

117 GEORGIAN CARVED AND GILDED EAGLE CONSOLE WITH INLAID MARBLE SLAB. The type shown by R. W. Symonds as originally accompanied by an architectural pier mirror with glass surmounted by a female mask such as those shown in 97 and 98.

118 EARLY GEORGIAN GILDED ARCHITECTURAL PIER MIRROR. Victoria & Albert Museum. Crown Copyright.

PLATE 92

119 EARLY GEORGIAN GILDED ARCHITECTURAL PIER MIRROR

PLATE 93

120 EARLY GEORGIAN GILDED ARCHITECTURAL PIER MIRROR

PLATE 94

121 EARLY GEORGIAN CARVED WALNUT PIER TABLE. Combining typical low-relief foliage carving as in the base of 122.

PLATE 95

122 EARLY GEORGIAN CARVED PINE ARCHITECTURAL PIER MIRROR

PLATE 96

123 EARLY GEORGIAN GILDED ARCHITECTURAL PIER MIRROR. With drapery-cord-and-tassel pendants.

PLATE 97

124 CHIPPENDALE GILDED ARCHITECTURAL PIER MIRROR

PLATE 98

125 GEORGE III CARVED PINE ARCHITECTURAL PIER MIRROR. With original label of "Kearney, Carver, Gilder and Looking Glass Maker to His Majesty." *Vide* also Oliver Brackett, *English Furniture, Illustrated,* 186.

126 GEORGE III GILDED ARCHITECTURAL PIER MIRROR. With label of Cornelius Callaghan, 24 Clare Street, Dublin. Courtesy of Christie, Manson & Woods, London.

PLATE 100

127 CHIPPENDALE MAHOGANY ARCHITECTURAL FRAME WITH BAROMETER, THERMOMETER, HYGROMETER AND A PERPETUAL REGULATION OF TIME PUBLISHED BY JOHN ALMENT, MARY'S ABBEY, DUBLIN, 1773. London versions appeared exactly twenty years earlier, calibrated from 1753 to 1852. *Vide* also Oliver Brackett, *English Furniture, Illustrated*, Fig. 362.

128 EARLY GEORGIAN CARVED AND PARCEL-GILDED GIRANDOLE MIRROR

129 EARLY GEORGIAN CARVED AND PARCEL-GILDED OVERMANTEL MIRROR

PLATE 102

130 EARLY GEORGIAN INLAID BURL WALNUT SECRETAIRE. With especially identifying coved stellate inlay and pedimental scrolls shaped like those of 131. Original Dublin ormoluwork. Victoria & Albert Museum. Crown Copyright.

131 EARLY GEORGIAN PARCEL-GILDED WALNUT PIER MIRROR

PLATE 104

132 EARLY GEORGIAN PARCEL-GILDED MAHOGANY PIER MIRROR. Exhibited as *in the Dutch style, English XVIII Century.*
Metropolitan Museum of Art.

PLATE 105

133 EARLY GEORGIAN PARCEL-GILDED WALNUT PIER MIRROR

PLATE 106

134 EARLY GEORGIAN PARCEL-GILDED EAGLE-HEAD ARMCHAIR. The eagle-head theme also of Dublin card (77), and pier tables and wall mirrors: 78, 85, 92-94, 108, 113, 114, 144, 161, 180.

PLATE 107

135 EARLY GEORGIAN PARCEL-GILDED MAHOGANY ARCHITECTURAL PIER MIRROR. Exhibited as *in the Kent Style, English*, circa 1725-1730. Metropolitan Museum of Art.

PLATE 108

136 EARLY GEORGIAN CARVED MAHOGANY ARCHITECTURAL CABINET. The specially hinged full-width cupboard door faced with a mirror plate and flanking pilasters surmounted by crisply carved leafy capitals resembling those of 135.

137 EARLY GEORGIAN PARCEL-GILDED WALNUT ARCHITECTURAL PIER MIRROR

PLATE 110

138 GEORGIAN CARVED MAHOGANY SECRETAIRE. The upper door panels scrolled and cusped as in the shapings of looking glasses such as 139.

139 GEORGIAN PARCEL-GILDED WALNUT LOOKING GLASS

PLATE 112

140 GEORGIAN PARCEL-GILDED WALNUT LOOKING GLASS

PLATE 113

141 GEORGIAN PARCEL-GILDED WALNUT PIER MIRROR. Victoria & Albert Museum. Crown Copyright.

PLATE 114

142 CHIPPENDALE PARCEL-GILDED MAHOGANY PIER MIRROR. Exhibited as *American, XVIII Century*. Metropolitan Museum of Art.

143 CHIPPENDALE PARCEL-GILDED MAHOGANY GIRANDOLE MIRROR. With especially characteristic pedimental treatment, rococo glass surround, and original ormolu candle arms.

PLATE 115

144 GEORGIAN PARCEL-GILDED WALNUT PIER MIRROR. With eagle heads and Prince-of-Wales plumes.

145 GEORGIAN PARCEL-GILDED MAHOGANY PIER MIRROR. With Prince-of-Wales plumes.

141

PLATE 116

146 EARLY FEDERAL GOUACHE DRAWING OF THE FRIGATE *UNITED STATES* Circa 1794. The ensigns denoting trade with countries reaching from Ireland to China, and continental cities from Hamburg to Leghorn. This insertion serves as a divider between designs of Dublin trade mirrors usually delivered throughout Great Britain, and those more frequently received in the American colonies and states.

PLATE 117

147 CHIPPENDALE PARCEL-GILDED WALNUT PIER MIRROR. Sold as American by an old-time importing dealer in Americana.

148 CHIPPENDALE PARCEL-GILDED WALNUT PIER MIRROR. Sold as American by a rival importer.

PLATE 118

149 CHIPPENDALE PARCEL-GILDED WALNUT PIER MIRROR.
Sold as American.

150 NORTH AMERICAN PINE FRAMEWORK AND
BACKBOARDS OF 149

PLATE 119

151 CHIPPENDALE PARCEL-GILDED WALNUT "CONSTITUTION" MIRROR

152 CHIPPENDALE PARCEL-GILDED WALNUT "CONSTITUTION" MIRROR. From the Hatfield family, Red Bank, New Jersey. From the Haskell Collection of Americana.

145

PLATE 120

153 CHIPPENDALE PARCEL-GILDED WALNUT PIER MIRROR. Sold as English.

154 CHIPPENDALE PARCEL-GILDED MAHOGANY "WASHINGTON" MIRROR. Sold as American.

PLATE 121

155 CHIPPENDALE PARCEL-GILDED WALNUT PIER MIRROR.
Sold as American.

156 CHIPPENDALE PARCEL-GILDED WALNUT PIER MIRROR.
Courtesy of J. J. Wolff (Antiques) Ltd., New York City.

147

PLATE 122

157 LATER GEORGIAN PARCEL-GILDED WALNUT "CONSTITUTION" MIRROR

158 LATER GEORGIAN PARCEL-GILDED MAHOGANY PIER MIRROR. Exhibited as *American, 1750-1775*. Metropolitan Museum of Art.

PLATE 123

159 LATER GEORGIAN PARCEL-GILDED MAHOGANY "PHILADELPHIA" MIRROR. Sold by an old-time importing dealer in Americana.

160 HEPPLEWHITE PARCEL-GILDED MAHOGANY "AMERICAN" PIER MIRROR

149

PLATE 124

161 CHIPPENDALE PARCEL-GILDED MAHOGANY "PHILADELPHIA" MIRROR

162 CHIPPENDALE PARCEL-GILDED MAHOGANY LOOKING GLASS. Victoria & Albert Museum. Crown Copyright.

PLATE 125

163 CHIPPENDALE PARCEL-GILDED MAHOGANY "PHILADELPHIA" MIRROR

164 CHIPPENDALE PARCEL-GILDED MAHOGANY PIER MIRROR WITH "PHILADELPHIA" URN FINIAL.
Cf 162-163, 167.

PLATE 126

165 CHIPPENDALE PARCEL-GILDED MAHOGANY LOOKING GLASS. Courtesy of Needham's Antiques, Inc., New York City.

166 CHIPPENDALE PARCEL-GILDED MAHOGANY LOOKING GLASS. With Prince-of-Wales plumes and motto "Ich Dien."

PLATE 127

167 CHIPPENDALE PARCEL-GILDED MAHOGANY "PHILADELPHIA" MIRROR

168 CHIPPENDALE PARCEL-GILDED MAHOGANY PIER MIRROR. Victoria & Albert Museum. Crown Copyright.

PLATE 128

169 CHIPPENDALE PARCEL-GILDED MAHOGANY
LOOKING GLASS. From an old-time London dealer.

170 CHIPPENDALE PARCEL-GILDED WALNUT LOOKING
GLASS. From an old-time importing dealer in Americana.

PLATE 129

171 CHIPPENDALE PARCEL-GILDED WALNUT LOOKING GLASS

172 CHIPPENDALE PARCEL-GILDED MAHOGANY LOOKING GLASS. Courtesy of Needham's Antiques, Inc., New York City.

155

PLATE 130

173 "EARLY FEDERAL" PARCEL-GILDED MAHOGANY LOOKING GLASS

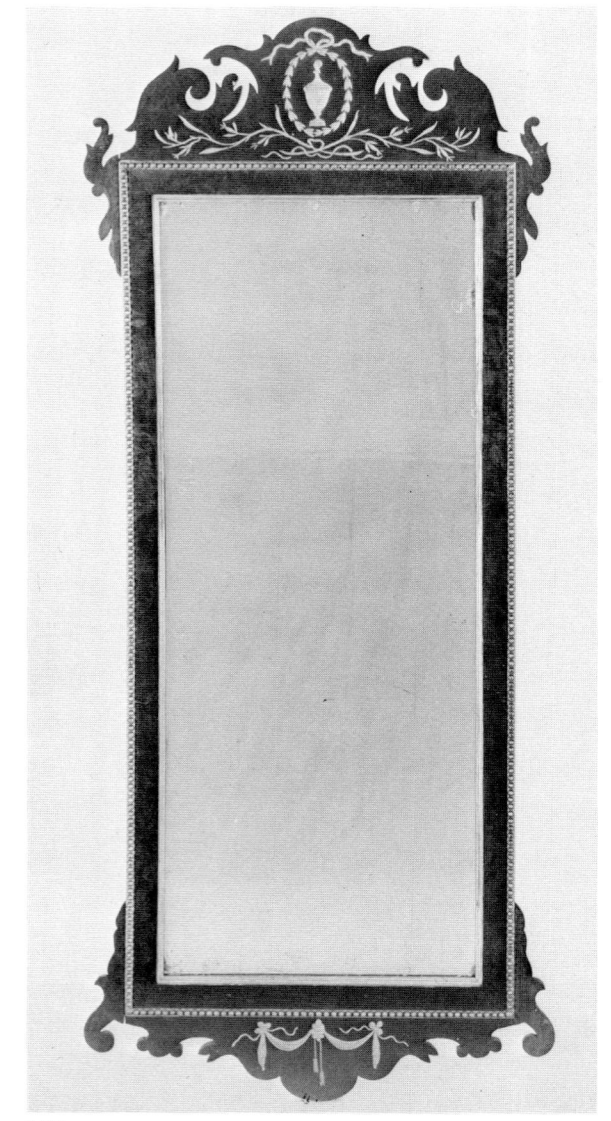

174 HEPPLEWHITE PARCEL-GILDED MAHOGANY PIER MIRROR. Collection of Luther Woodbury, Beverly, Massachusetts.

PLATE 131

175 GEORGIAN PARCEL-GILDED MAHOGANY LOOKING GLASS. Victoria & Albert Museum. Crown Copyright.

176 HEPPLEWHITE PARCEL-GILDED MAHOGANY LOOKING GLASS

PLATE 132

177 CHIPPENDALE PARCEL-GILDED MAHOGANY "NEW YORK" MIRROR

178 CHIPPENDALE PARCEL-GILDED MAHOGANY "NEW YORK" LOOKING GLASS

PLATE 133

179 CHIPPENDALE PARCEL-GILDED MAHOGANY
"NEW YORK" LOOKING GLASS

180 GEORGIAN PARCEL-GILDED MAHOGANY
EAGLE-HEAD MIRROR

PLATE 134

181 "EARLY FEDERAL" PARCEL-GILDED MAHOGANY PIER MIRROR

182 "CHIPPENDALE" PARCEL-GILDED MAHOGANY LOOKING GLASS. Sold as American or English.

PLATE 135

184 "CHIPPENDALE" PARCEL-GILDED MAHOGANY OVAL LOOKING GLASS. Exhibited as *New York, Third Quarter XVIII Century*. Metropolitan Museum of Art.

183 "CHIPPENDALE" PARCEL-GILDED MAHOGANY LOOKING GLASS. Sold as American.

161

PLATE 136

185 GEORGIAN PARCEL-GILDED MAHOGANY LOOKING GLASS. Exhibited as *American XVIII Century*. Metropolitan Museum of Art.

186 GEORGIAN PARCEL-GILDED MAHOGANY LOOKING GLASS. With Prince-of-Wales plumes.

PLATE 137

187 HEPPLEWHITE INLAID AND PARCEL-GILDED
"BOSTON" OVAL LOOKING GLASS

188 HEPPLEWHITE PARCEL-GILDED MAHOGANY
LOOKING GLASS. Exhibited as *American 1790-1800*.
Metropolitan Museum of Art.

163

PLATE 138

189 HEPPLEWHITE PARCEL-GILDED MAHOGANY "AMERICAN" MIRROR WITH EGLOMISÉ PANEL

190 HEPPLEWHITE INLAID AND PARCEL-GILDED MAHOGANY "NEW YORK" MIRROR

PLATE 139

191 HEPPLEWHITE INLAID AND PARCEL-GILDED MAHOGANY "NEW YORK" MIRROR

192 HEPPLEWHITE INLAID AND PARCEL-GILDED MAHOGANY "NEW YORK" MIRROR. With eglomisé panel depicting an Irish rustic landscape. (Skirting replaced).

165

PLATE 140

193 CHIPPENDALE CARVED AND GILDED WALL BRACKET. One of a pair acquired in Munich, Bavaria.

194 CHIPPENDALE CARVED AND GILDED "AMERICAN" WALL BRACKET

PLATE 141

195 CHIPPENDALE CARVED AND GILDED WALL BRACKET

196 CHIPPENDALE CARVED AND GILDED GIRANDOLE.
Courtesy of Charles Lumb & Sons Ltd., Harrogate.

PLATE 142

197 CHIPPENDALE CARVED AND GILDED CARTEL.
Movement by John Perins, London.

198 CHIPPENDALE CARVED AND GILDED ÉTAGERE.
Courtesy of French & Co., Inc., New York City.

199 CHIPPENDALE CARVED AND GILDED GIRANDOLE

PLATE 144

200 CHIPPENDALE MAHOGANY UPHOLSTERED SETTEE. With frilled edging more characteristic of mirror carvings, the legs distinctively enhanced with oak leaves and acorns. Exhibited as *English*, circa *1750*. Metropolitan Museum of Art.

PLATE 145

201 CHIPPENDALE CARVED AND GILDED WALL MIRROR. Courtesy of Asprey & Company Limited, London.

PLATE 146

202 CHIPPENDALE CARVED AND GILDED WALL MIRROR.
Courtesy of J. J. Wolff (Antiques) Ltd., New York City.

203 CHIPPENDALE CARVED AND GILDED WALL MIRROR.
Courtesy of J. J. Wolff (Antiques) Ltd., New York City.

PLATE 147

204 CHIPPENDALE CARVED AND GILDED WALL MIRROR

205 CHIPPENDALE CARVED AND GILDED WALL MIRROR.
Courtesy of J. J. Wolff (Antiques) Ltd., New York City.

173

PLATE 148

206 CHIPPENDALE CARVED AND GILDED WALL MIRROR.
Courtesy of Charles Lumb & Sons Ltd., Harrogate.

207 CHIPPENDALE CARVED AND GILDED WALL MIRROR.
Courtesy of Charles Lumb & Sons Ltd., Harrogate.

PLATE 149

208 CHIPPENDALE CARVED AND GILDED WALL MIRROR.
Courtesy of J. J. Wolff (Antiques) Ltd., New York City.

209 CHIPPENDALE CARVED AND GILDED WALL MIRROR.
Courtesy of J. J. Wolff (Antiques) Ltd., New York City.

PLATE 150

210 CHIPPENDALE CARVED AND GILDED WALL MIRROR.
Courtesy of J. J. Wolff (Antiques) Ltd., New York City.

211 CHIPPENDALE CARVED AND GILDED WALL MIRROR.
Courtesy of Charles Lumb & Sons Ltd., Harrogate.

PLATE 151

213 CHIPPENDALE CARVED AND GILDED WALL MIRROR.
Courtesy of Charles Lumb & Sons Ltd., Harrogate.

212 CHIPPENDALE CARVED AND GILDED WALL MIRROR.
Courtesy of Charles Lumb & Sons Ltd., Harrogate.

PLATE 152

214 CHIPPENDALE CARVED AND GILDED PIER MIRROR. Courtesy of Needham's Antiques, Inc., New York City.

215 CHIPPENDALE CARVED AND GILDED WALL MIRROR

PLATE 153

216   CHIPPENDALE CARVED AND GILDED FRAME WITH CHINESE MIRROR PAINTING

PLATE 154

217 CHIPPENDALE CARVED AND GILDED WALL MIRROR. At Powerscourt, County Wicklow.
Courtesy of the late Noel C. Hartnell, Dublin.

PLATE 155

218 CHIPPENDALE CARVED AND GILDED FRAME WITH CHINESE MIRROR PAINTING

PLATE 156

219 CHINESE-CHIPPENDALE LACQUER-DECORATED BEDSTEAD MADE FOR BADMINTON HOUSE, GLOUCESTERSHIRE. Authoritatively but erroneously claimed as the work of Chippendale, and also as that of the Linnells. The distinctive Dublin dragon finials might be considered as unique, except that they appear also in 220, claimed as German. Victoria & Albert Museum. Crown Copyright.

PLATE 157

220 CHINESE-CHIPPENDALE LACQUER-DECORATED WALL MIRROR EN SUITE WITH THE DESIGN OF THE BADMINTON BEDSTEAD. Exhibited as German. *Vide* also Percy Macquoid, *Age of Satinwood*, Fig. 8; another closely related example, made in Dublin for the Duke of Beaufort, Badminton House, *Gloucestershire*. Victoria & Albert Museum. Crown Copyright.

PLATE 158

221   CHINESE-CHIPPENDALE CARVED AND GILDED WALL MIRROR

PLATE 159

222 CHIPPENDALE CARVED AND GILDED WALL MIRROR. Attributed to Thomas Johnson. From Tyrone House, Dublin. Courtesy of the late Noel C. Hartnell, Dublin.

PLATE 160

223 CHIPPENDALE CARVED AND GILDED GIRANDOLE MIRROR. Exhibited as *Probably by Chippendale, About 1760*. The slanted positioning and the overflashing of this specially photographed frame has not too seriously marred its presentation here—in combination with the following example—as representative of Dublin designs that have no close counterparts in any recognizable London productions. Victoria & Albert Museum. Crown Copyright.

PLATE 161

224 CHIPPENDALE CARVED AND GILDED GIRANDOLE MIRROR. Exhibited as *Probably by Chippendale*. Victoria & Albert Museum. Crown Copyright.

225 CHIPPENDALE CARVED AND GILDED WALL MIRROR

226 CHIPPENDALE CARVED AND GILDED PIER MIRROR. Metropolitan Museum of Art.

PLATE 164

227 CHIPPENDALE CARVED AND GILDED OVAL WALL MIRROR. Courtesy of J. J. Wolff (Antiques) Ltd., New York City.

228 CHIPPENDALE CARVED AND GILDED OVAL WALL MIRROR. Courtesy of Charles Lumb & Sons Ltd., Harrogate.

PLATE 165

229 CHIPPENDALE CARVED AND GILDED OVAL WALL MIRROR. With "Philadelphia" urn finial.

230 CHIPPENDALE CARVED AND GILDED OVAL WALL MIRROR. Courtesy of Biggs of Maidenhead.

PLATE 166

231 CHIPPENDALE CARVED AND GILDED OVAL WALL MIRROR. Courtesy of J. J. Wolff (Antiques) Ltd., New York City.

232 CHIPPENDALE CARVED AND GILDED OVAL WALL MIRROR

PLATE 167

233 CHIPPENDALE CARVED AND GILDED OVAL PIER MIRROR. Courtesy of Asprey & Company Limited, London.

PLATE 168

234 CHIPPENDALE CARVED AND GILDED OVAL WALL MIRROR

235 CHIPPENDALE CARVED AND GILDED OVAL WALL MIRROR

PLATE 169

236 CHIPPENDALE CARVED AND GILDED OVAL WALL MIRROR

PLATE 170

237 CHIPPENDALE CARVED AND GILDED OVAL WALL MIRROR. Courtesy of J. J. Wolff (Antiques) Ltd., New York City.

238 CHIPPENDALE CARVED AND GILDED OVAL WALL MIRROR. Courtesy of J. J. Wolff (Antiques) Ltd., New York City.

239 LATE CHIPPENDALE CARVED AND GILDED PIER MIRROR. Courtesy of Asprey & Company Limited, London.

PLATE 172

240 LATE CHIPPENDALE CARVED AND GILDED OVAL
WALL MIRROR. Courtesy of Charles Lumb & Sons
Ltd., Harrogate.

241 LATE CHIPPENDALE CARVED AND GILDED OVAL
WALL MIRROR

242 LATE CHIPPENDALE CARVED AND GILDED OVAL WALL MIRROR. Courtesy of Asprey & Company Limited, London.

243 HEPPLEWHITE CARVED AND GILDED OVAL WALL MIRROR

PLATE 174

244 HEPPLEWHITE GILDED OVAL PIER MIRROR

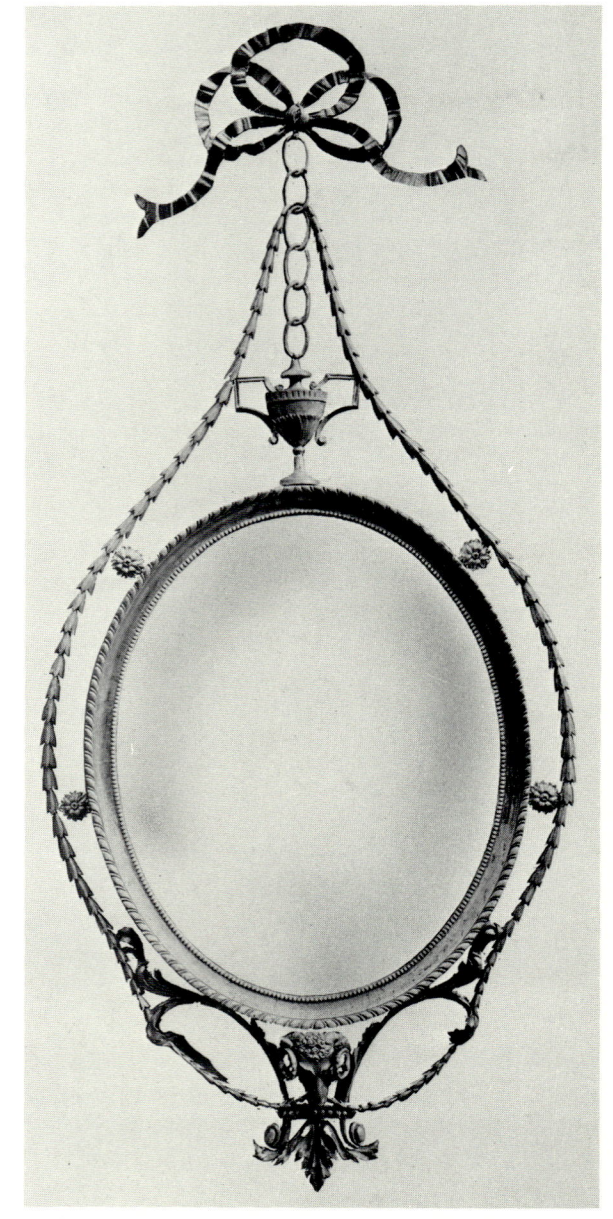

245 HEPPLEWHITE GILDED OVAL PIER MIRROR

PLATE 175

246 HEPPLEWHITE GILDED OVAL PIER MIRROR. With Prince-of-Wales Plumes.

PLATE 176

247 HEPPLEWHITE GILDED OVAL WALL MIRROR.
With eglomisé medallion. Authoritatively viewed as
Possibly Danish.

248 HEPPLEWHITE GILDED OVAL WALL MIRROR. With
eglomisé cupid medallion. Expertized as *Scandinavian.*

PLATE 177

249 HEPPLEWHITE GILDED OVERMANTEL MIRROR. With eglomisé panel.

PLATE 178

250 HEPPLEWHITE GILDED GIRANDOLE WITH DRAPERY APPLIQUE

251 HEPPLEWHITE GILDED OVAL PIER MIRROR. With favorite cord-and-tassel festoons.

PLATE 180

252 HEPPLEWHITE GILDED OVAL PIER MIRROR.
Courtesy of Biggs of Maidenhead.

253 HEPPLEWHITE GILDED OVAL PIER MIRROR.
With Prince-of-Wales plumes.

PLATE 181

254 HEPPLEWHITE GILDED OVAL PIER MIRROR.
With blue-painted and gilded figural medallion.

255 HEPPLEWHITE GILDED PIER MIRROR.
With mirror-plate border and figural medallion.

PLATE 182

256 EARLY GEORGIAN GILDED MIRROR WITH HEPPLEWHITE ADDITIONS.

257 HEPPLEWHITE GILDED "AMERICAN" MIRROR

208

PLATE 183

258 HEPPLEWHITE GILDED "AMERICAN" MIRROR

259 HEPPLEWHITE GILDED "AMERICAN" MIRROR

PLATE 184

260 HEPPLEWHITE GILDED PIER MIRROR.
With Prince-of-Wales plumes.

261 HEPPLEWHITE GILDED "AMERICAN" MIRROR

PLATE 185

263 HEPPLEWHITE GILDED WALL MIRROR. Sold as American by an old-time importing dealer in Americana.

262 HEPPLEWHITE GILDED WALL MIRROR. Exhibited as *American, Late XVIII Century.* Cf cresting of 275. Metropolitan Museum of Art.

PLATE 186

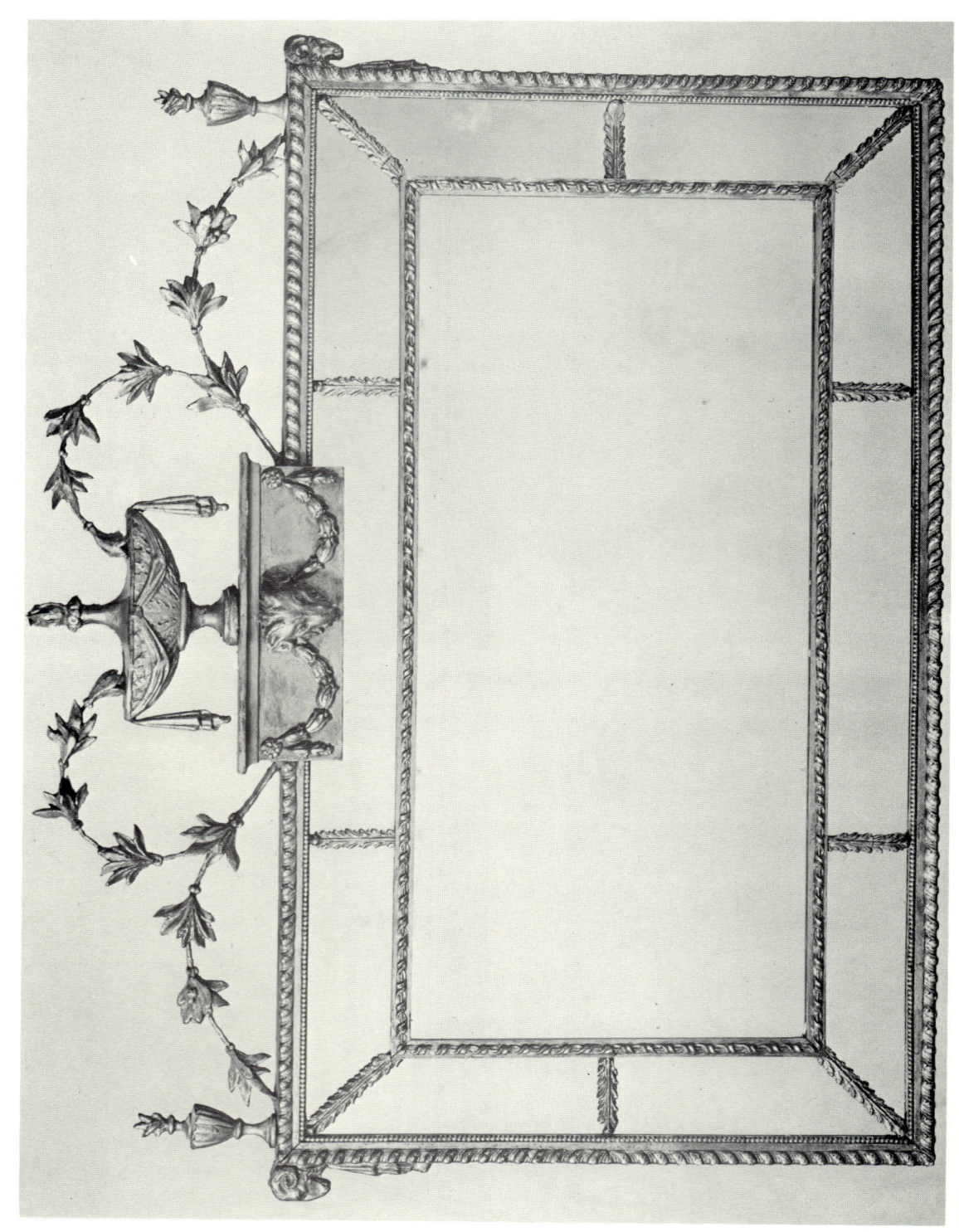

264 SHERATON GILDED OVERMANTEL MIRROR WITH SEGMENTAL PLATE BORDER. Sold as *Adam*, *English XVIII Century*. Cf urn finials of 265.

PLATE 187

265 SHERATON GILDED WALL MIRROR WITH EGLOMISÉ PANEL. Courtesy of French & Co., Inc., New York City.

PLATE 188

266 SHERATON GILDED "ENGLISH" WALL MIRROR WITH EGLOMISÉ PANEL

267 SHERATON GILDED "AMERICAN" WALL MIRROR WITH EGLOMISÉ PANEL

PLATE 189

268 SHERATON GILDED PIER MIRROR WITH EGLOMISÉ PANELS

PLATE 190

269 SHERATON GILDED WALL MIRROR WITH PORTRAIT ENGRAVING OF WASHINGTON. With distributor's label, "James Stokes, Philadelphia."

270 SHERATON GILDED WALL MIRROR WITH EGLOMISÉ PANEL COMMEMORATIVE OF G. WASHINGTON. Found in England.

PLATE 191

271 SHERATON GILDED WALL MIRROR WITH PORTRAIT ENGRAVING OF G. WASHINGTON, ESQ. From the Van Rensselaer family of New York.

PLATE 192

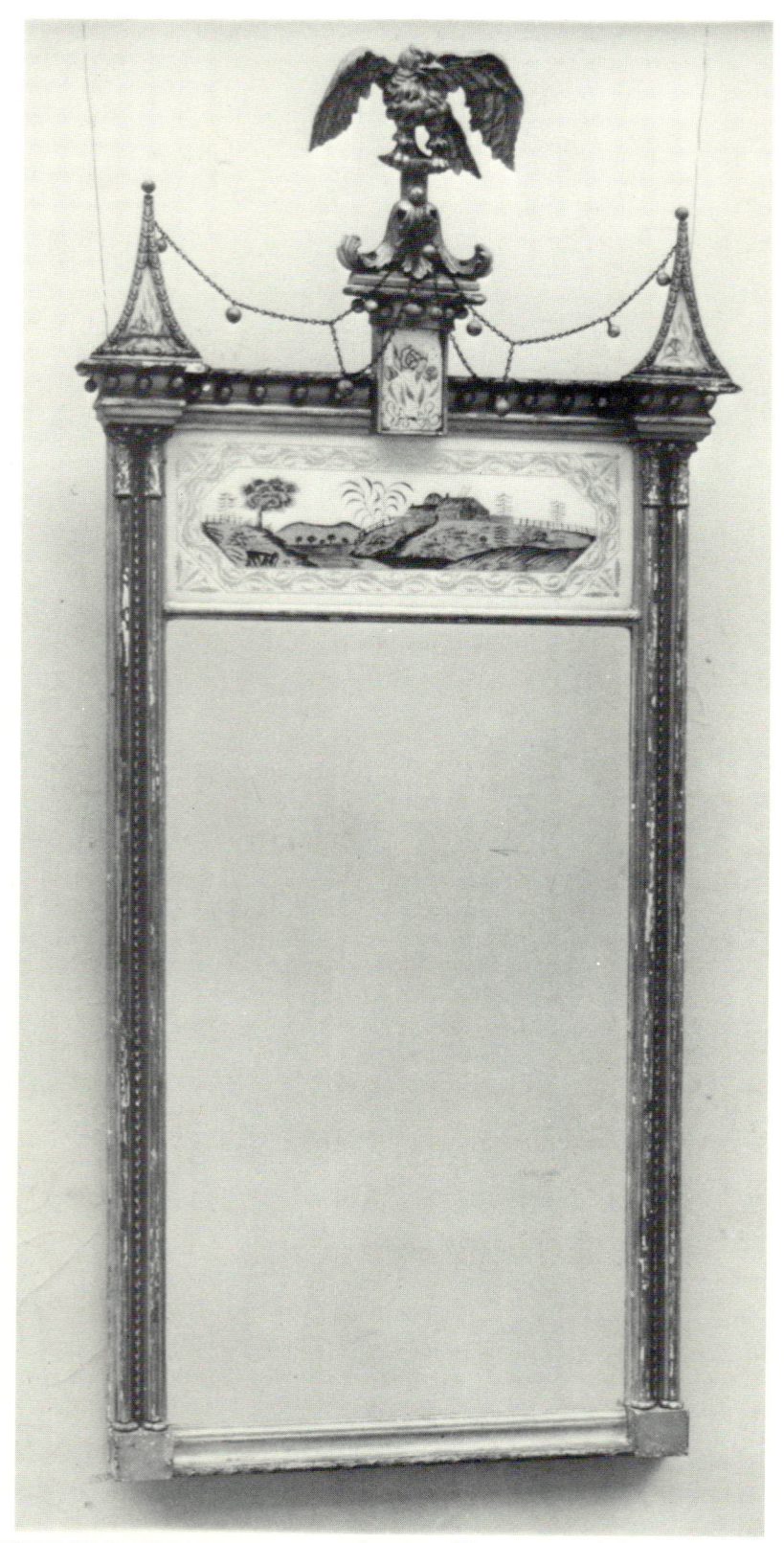

272 SHERATON GILDED WALL MIRROR WITH EGLOMISÉ PANELS. The main panel depicting an Irish country landscape. Exhibited as *New York, 1790-1800*. Metropolitan Museum of Art.

PLATE 193

273 SHERATON GILDED PIER MIRROR WITH EGLOMISÉ PANELS. Courtesy of Joe Kindig, Jr., York, Pennsylvania.

PLATE 194

274 SHERATON GILDED PIER MIRROR. The eglomisé panel depicting an Irish country scene with rustic cottages.

PLATE 195

275 SHERATON GILDED PIER MIRROR WITH EGLOMISÉ PANEL. Cf 262.

PLATE 196

276 SHERATON GILDED OVERMANTEL MIRROR WITH EGLOMISÉ PANELS

277 SHERATON GILDED PIER MIRROR WITH EGLOMISÉ PANELS

PLATE 198

278 SHERATON GILDED OVERMANTEL MIRROR WITH EGLOMISÉ PANELS. Exhibited as *American*, circa 1800.

279 SHERATON GILDED OVERMANTEL MIRROR WITH EGLOMISÉ PANELS

PLATE 199

280 REGENCY GILDED OVERMANTEL MIRROR. Supposedly made by Samuel McIntyre, Salem, Massachusetts. From the Wadsworth Family, Salem, Massachusetts.

PLATE 200

281 REGENCY GILDED OVERMANTEL MIRROR WITH EAGLE SCONCES. Courtesy of J. J. Wolff (Antiques) Ltd., New York City.

PLATE 201

284 REGENCY GILDED GIRANDOLE. Exhibited as *English, XVIII Century*. Metropolitan Museum of Art.

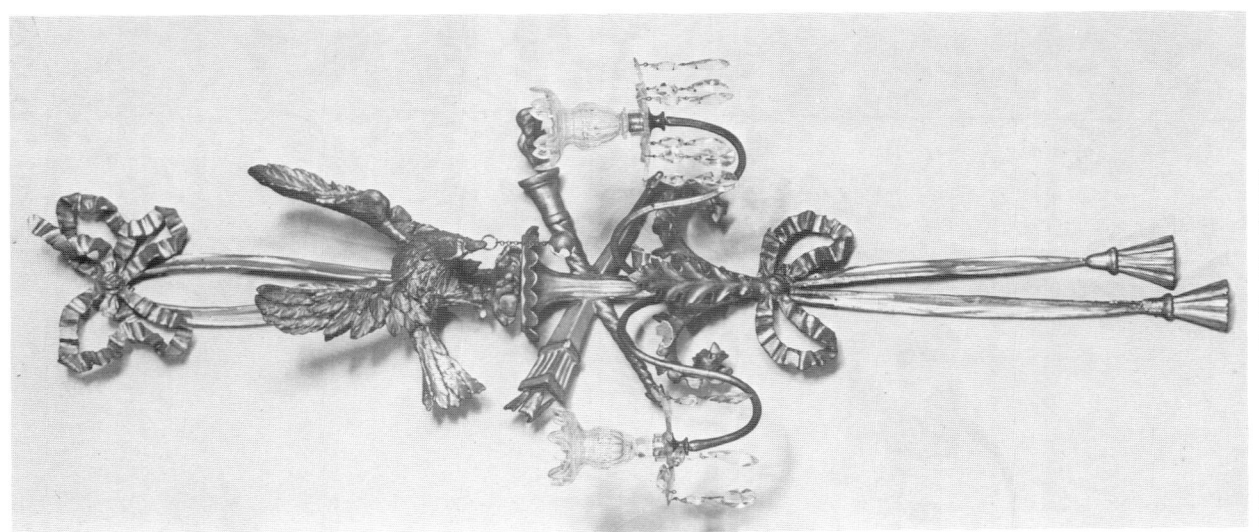

283 SHERATON GILDED GIRANDOLE. With Irish glass fittings.

282 LATE GEORGIAN GILDED GIRANDOLE

227

PLATE 202

285 REGENCY GILDED AND EBONIZED EAGLE GIRANDOLE

286 REGENCY GILDED AND EBONIZED EAGLE WALL MIRROR. Courtesy of J. J. Wolff (Antiques) Ltd., New York City.

PLATE 203

287 REGENCY GILDED CONVEX EAGLE WALL MIRROR. The ormolu candle arms with Irish glass fittings.

PLATE 204

288 REGENCY GILDED AND EBONIZED FIGURAL SCONCE

289 REGENCY GILDED AND EBONIZED CONVEX DOLPHIN WALL MIRROR

290 REGENCY GILDED CONVEX GIRANDOLE MIRROR WITH EGLOMISÉ BORDER. Courtesy of Charles Lumb & Sons Ltd., Harrogate.

PLATE 206

291 REGENCY GILDED AND EBONIZED "AMERICAN" CONVEX EAGLE WALL MIRROR. Collection of Charles N. Bancker, New York and Philadelphia, d. 1869. Collection of James Bancker, New York, d. 1897.

292 REGENCY GILDED AND EBONIZED CONVEX GIRANDOLE MIRROR.

293 REGENCY GILDED AND EBONIZED CONVEX GIRANDOLE MIRROR. With Irish glass fittings. Cf. 303. Exhibited as *American, Early XIX Century*. Metropolitan Museum of Art.

PLATE 208

294 REGENCY GILDED AND EBONIZED CONVEX EAGLE WALL MIRROR

295 REGENCY GILDED CONVEX EAGLE GIRANDOLE MIRROR

PLATE 209

296 REGENCY GILDED CONVEX EAGLE GIRANDOLE MIRROR. Courtesy of Biggs of Maidenhead.

297 REGENCY GILDED CONVEX EAGLE-AND-SERPENT GIRANDOLE MIRROR. Exhibited as *American, about 1790*. Metropolitan Museum of Art.

PLATE 210

298 REGENCY GILDED CONVEX EAGLE WALL MIRROR.
At Moore Abbey, County Kildare. Courtesy of the late
Noel C. Hartnell, Dublin.

299 VICTORIAN GILDED CONVEX EAGLE WALL MIRROR

PLATE 211

300 A THOROUGHLY CHARACTERISTIC DUTCH GILDED PIER MIRROR

301 LATE GEORGIAN GILDED SUNRAY FRAME, WITH CLOCK

237

PLATE 212

302 INSET SLAB OF 99. With specimen marbles.

PLATE 213

303 GEORGE III WATERFORD CUT GLASS CHANDELIERE WITH HURRICANE SHIELDS. *Vide* 293.
304 GEORGE III WATERFORD CUT GLASS, ORMOLU & DECORATED EMERALD-GREEN GLASS CANDELABRUM. Described as *English*.
305 GEORGE III IRISH CUT GLASS CANDELABRUM. Described as *English or Irish*.

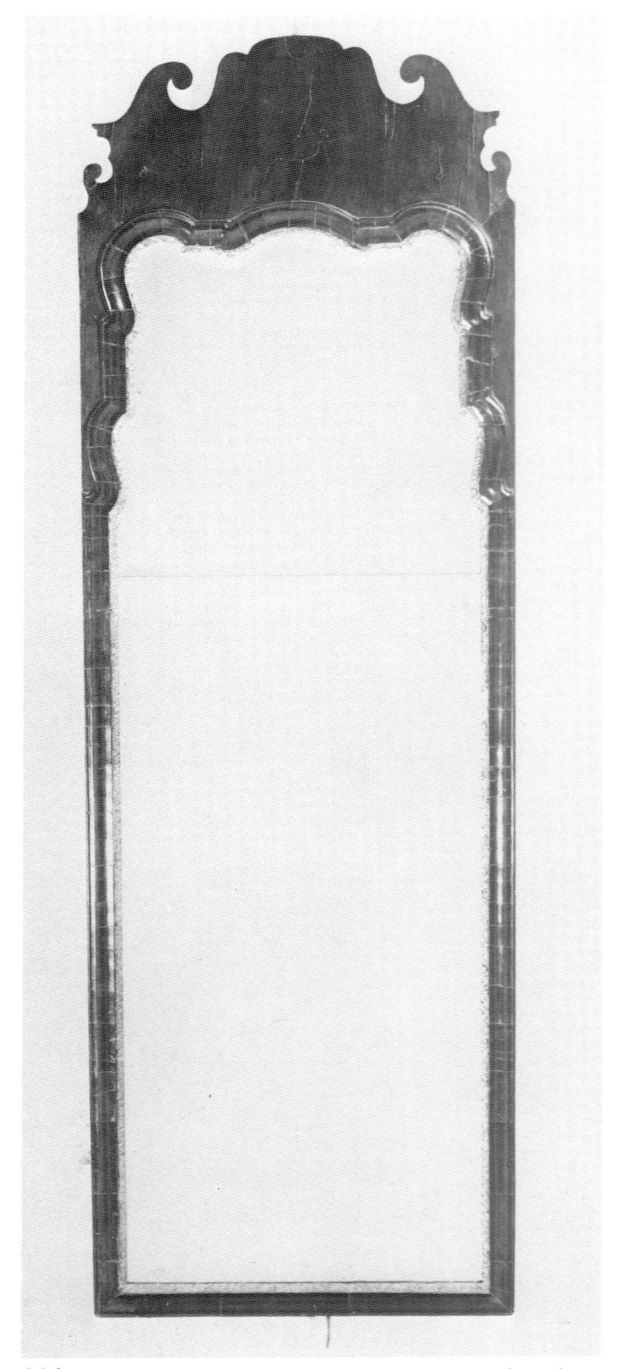

PLATE 214

SUPPLEMENTARY ILLUSTRATIONS

307 QUEEN ANNE PARCEL-GILDED MAHOGANY "PHILADELPHIA" MIRROR

306 QUEEN ANNE WALNUT PIER MIRROR. Attributed to John Elliott.

PLATE 215

308 GEORGIAN PARCEL-GILDED WALNUT "PHILADELPHIA" MIRROR. With Prince-of-Wales plumes.

309 GEORGIAN PARCEL-GILDED WALNUT "PHILADELPHIA" MIRROR. With Prince-of-Wales plumes.

241

PLATE 216

310 CHIPPENDALE PARCEL-GILDED WALNUT "CONSTITUTION" TYPE MIRROR. Courtesy of Needham's Antiques, Inc., New York City.

311 LATE GEORGIAN PARCEL-GILDED MAHOGANY LOOKING GLASS. Sold by an old-time importing dealer as *American, XVIII Century.*

PLATE 218

312 CHIPPENDALE PARCEL-GILDED MAHOGANY "AMERICAN" LOOKING GLASS

PLATE 219

313 CHIPPENDALE PARCEL-GILDED MAHOGANY PIER MIRROR. With distributor's label, "John Elliott, Philadelphia."

PLATE 220

314 GEORGIAN PARCEL-GILDED MAHOGANY PIER MIRROR. With winged cherub head. Cf. 90, 92.

315 GEORGIAN PARCEL-GILDED MAHOGANY PIER MIRROR. Exhibited as *American 1750-1775*. Metropolitan Museum of Art.

PLATE 221

316 CHIPPENDALE PARCEL-GILDED MAHOGANY "CONSTITUTION" MIRROR. Courtesy of Charles Lumb & Sons Ltd., Harrogate, England.

317 LATE GEORGIAN PARCEL-GILDED MAHOGANY PIER MIRROR. Exhibited as *American 1750-1775*. Vide finial of 184. Metropolitan Museum of Art.

PLATE 222

318 LATE GEORGIAN PARCEL-GILDED MAHOGANY LOOKING GLASS

PLATE 223

319 LATE GEORGIAN PARCEL-GILDED MAHOGANY
LOOKING GLASS. The type distributed *circa* 1790-1795
by William Wilmerding. Possibly the original,
damaged finial.

320 LATE GEORGIAN PARCEL-GILDED MAHOGANY
LOOKING GLASS

249

PLATE 224

321-322 CHIPPENDALE CARVED AND GILDED PIER MIRROR WITH EAGLE CONSOLE

Index

[Italic figures refer to illustrations]

Abies alba, 11
Abies nigra, 11
Adaptive ornamentation, *256*
Age of Satinwood, 17, *220*
Alment, John, *127*
America, Irish glass exported to, 9
America, looking glasses to, 23
American (misnomer), 9, 11, *15*, 16, *17*, 28, 29, 39, *129*, *142*, *147-150*, *154*, *155*, *158*, *160*, *185*, *187-189*, *257-259*, *261-263*, *267*, *278*, *291*, *293*, *297*, *311*, *312*, *315*, *317*
American colonists, 12, 23
American craftsmen, 11
American distributors of looking glasses, 21-23
American imports of Irish glasswares, 10
American nomenclature, 22
American pine, 11
American retailers of looking glasses, 21
American Revolution, 23
American spread eagle, *273*
American walnut, 11
American wholesalers of looking glasses, 21
Americana, collectors of, 16
Antiques, magazine, 16
Appliqué, *250*
Architectural commode, *51*
Armchair, *134*

Backboards, *150*
Backboards of mirror frames, 11
Backings of mirror plates, 10
Badminton House, 8, 17, *219*, *220*
Bancker, Charles N., *291*
Bancker, James, *291*
Barometer, *113*, *127*
Basin stand, *63*
Bateman, Viscount, 14, *71*
Beaufort, Duke of, 8, 18, *220*
Bedstead, *219*
Boston (misnomer), 11, *17*

Bowes, Sir William, *114*
Bracket, *193*, *194*, *195*
Brackett, Oliver, 17, *127*
Bramshill, 17
Breakage, of antique mirror plates, 10
British homes, 7
Bureau, dressing, *45*

Cabinet, *24*, *49*, *87*, *136*
Caliper measures of mirror plates, 10
Callahan, Cornelius, *126*
Canada pine, 11
Candelabrum, *304*, *305*
Carriages from Dublin to America, 9
Cartel, *197*
Cassiobury Park, 15
Cescinsky, Herbert, 15
Chandeliere, *303*
Chariot glasses, 9
Charles II (misnomer), 11, 15, *89*
Cherub head, *88*, *89*, *92*
Chest, *71*
Chest of drawers, *62*
Cheval glass, *64*
China, trade, *146*
Chinese bedroom at Badminton, 17
Chinese mirror painting, *216*, *218*
Chinese wallpaper, 17
Chippendale, Thomas, 8, 17, 18, *219*, *223*, *224*
Chippendale, Thomas, 17
Circa dates, 12
Coach glasses, 9
Cobham, Viscount, 17
Colored glass, 9
Commode, Dublin, *51*
Connoisseur, 14, 15
Console, eagle, *117*
Constitution mirrors, 12, 22, *151*, *152*, *157*, *310*, *311*, *316*

Continental furniture, 10
Continental timber buyers, 11
Corbeilles, 15
Cord-and-tassel, *94, 123, 251*
Cores of mirror frames, 11
Corner cupboard, *22*
Country landscape, *192, 272*
Crichel, 17
Crowns and coronets, 10
Cupboard, *22*

Danish (misnomer), *247*
Davis, Derek C., 8
Devonshire, Duke of, 15
Dictionary of English Furniture, 10, 12, 17
Director, Chippendale's, 8, 18
Director style, 17
Directory of the Historic Cabinet Woods, 11
Distributors of looking glasses, 21-23
Dolphin, *289*
Dorset, 17
Drapery-cord-and-tassel, *123*
Dublin, *126, 127*
Dublin carriages to America, 9
Dublin Castle, 9
Dublin coach glasses to America, 9
Dublin colored glass, 9
Dublin escutcheon, 13
Dublin exports throughout the British Isles, 9
Dublin exports to America, 9
Dublin glass, 9
Dublin lacquer skills, 11
Dublin tapestry, 15
Dublin tax-free port, 7
Dublin's commercial ascendancy over London, 23
Dutch (misnomer), *7, 10, 12, 16, 19, 23, 36, 132*
"Dutch manner" painting, 12
Dutch mirror, authentic, *300*
Dutch Style (misnomer), 16, *132*
Duties on English glass, 7
Duty-free Irish glass, 7

Eagle, *89, 117, 130*
Eagle console, 23
Eagle-head armchair, *134*
Eagle-head mirror, 180
Eagle sconces, *281*
Eagle, spread, *273*
Eagles and eagle heads, 14, *77, 93, 134, 144, 180*
Early Federal mirror, *173, 181, 183*
Early Federal trade, *146*
Edinburgh, 22
Edwards & Jourdain, 8n.1, 17, 19nn.1, 5, 6
Edwards, Richard, 16
Elliott advertisements, 21
Elliott imports, 12
Eliott, John, 11, 12, 16, 21, 22, *41, 306, 313*

Elliott-labeled mirror, 22
English (misnomer), 11, 13, 19, *25, 43, 114, 130, 132, 135, 200, 264, 266, 270, 284*
English and Irish Antique Glass, 8
English counties, 23
English furniture (misnomer), 14
English Furniture, Illustrated, 127
English Furniture Making in the 17th and 18th Century, 15
Etagere, *198*
Excise Act of 1745, 7
Excise taxes, 23

Fox, Morris, 10
Fraudulently labeled piece, 14
Free Trade, in Dublin, etc., 8
Free trading rights, 9
Frigate *United States, 146*

George II, 15
Georgian cabinetmakers, 7, 13, 17
German (misnomer), 17, *219, 220*
Glass chandelieres, 7, 9
Glass colored, 9
Glass, domestic (household), 7
Glass exports to America, 9
Glass makers, emigrate from England, 7
Glass, window, 9
Glasses, chariot and coach, 9
Glasses, drinking, 9
Glasses, imported by the Elliotts, 21
Glasses, reused looking, 9
Glasshouse, Waterford, 9
Glassworks, Irish, 7
Glassworks shut down in England, 7
Gloucestershire, 8, 17
Gouache drawing, *146*
Granger, Hugh, 13, 14
Griffiths, Percival, 10
Guiness, Desmond, 19n.7

Hagley Hall, 17
Hamburg, *146*
Hampshire, 17
Handles, Dublin, *51*
Haskell collection of Americana, *152*
Heraldic bearings, 10
Holland (misnomer), 10
Houghton Hall, 15
Hudson River views, 19
Hurricane shields, *293, 303*
Hygrometer, *127*
Hyndford, Earl of, 15

"Ich Dien," *166*
Importing dealer in Americana, *159, 170, 263, 311*
Independence Hall, 9
Inlaid marble, *99, 117, 302*

Index

Inset marble slab, *95, 99, 302*
Insurance claims, 10
Irish castles and mansions, 9
Irish country landscapes, 19, *192, 272, 274*
Irish glass exported to America, 9
Irish glass exported to England, 9
Irish glass exported to West Indies, 9
Irish glass fittings, *283, 287, 293*
Irish Houses and Castles, 19n.7
Irish residences, 19
Irish tapestry, 15

Johnson, Thomas, 18, *222*

Kearney, Joshua, 15
Kearney, To His Majesty, *125*
Knot-free pine, 11

Label, *125, 269, 313*
Lamp bracket, *86, 113*
Lead in mirror plates, 10
Leghorn, *146*
Leigh, Lord, 17
Linnells, 17
Linnells, the, 17, *219*
Little, Tennyson, 9
Liverpool, 11
Lizotte Glass, 10
Lizotte, L. P., 10
London, 7, 11
London glassworks, 7
London market, 7, 12, 15
London techniques of design, 13
London, vessels from, 12
Longford Castle, 15

Macquoid, Percy, 17, *220*
Marble, Irish, 15
Marble slabs, 15
Marble top, inlaid, *99, 117, 302*
Marble top, inset, *95, 99, 302*
Marbles, specimen, *99, 302*
Marnoch, J. N. O., 22
Mary's Abbey, *127*
Massachusetts (misnomer), 11, *16,* 280
McIntire, Samuel, 19, *280*
Mercury-back mirror plates, 10
Metropolitan Mirror & Glass Co., 10
Metropolitan Museum, 12, 16
Mirror backboards, 11
Mirror frames remade, 9
Mirror plates, thicknesses, 10
Moldings, classification by, 14
Moore Abbey, *298*
Munich, *193*

New York, *319*
New York (misnomer), 19, *177, 178, 179, 184, 190, 191, 192*

North American pine, 11
North American white pine, *150*

Oil painting, *68*
Old English Furniture (misnomer), 16

Paris, 19
Perpetual regulation of time, *127*
Perrins, John, *197*
Philadelphia, 11, 12, 14, 21, 22, *269*
Philadelphia (misnomer), *27, 32, 159, 161, 163, 167, 307, 308, 309*
Philadelphia Chippendale style (misnomer), 16
Philadelphia furniture designs, 12, 14
"Philadelphia" urn finial, *164, 229*
Pier tables, *91, 95, 96, 99, 101, 105, 107, 109, 111, 121*
Pierce Nichols home, 19
Pine, American, 11
Pine, Canadian, 11
Pine, knot-free, 11
Pine, North American, 11, *150*
Pine, yellow, 11
Pine, white, 11
Pinus abies, 11
Pinus strobus, 11
Pocock, Dr., 8, 17, 18
Powerscourt, 14, *217*
Prince-of-Wales, motto of, *166*
Prince-of-Wales plumes, 12, *144, 145, 166, 186, 246, 253, 260, 308, 309*

Red Lacquer Mirror, A, 14
Rogers, John, 14
Rustic landscape, Irish, *192, 272, 274*
Ryan, William, 19n.7

St. Giles House, 17
Salem, 19
Salem (misnomer), *280*
Scandinavian (misnomer), *248*
Secretaire, *23, 130, 138*
Settee, *200*
Shaftesbury, Earl of, 17
Shaving mirror, *63*
Ships from London, 21
Shropshire, 23
Silver nitrate, 10
Silvering of mirror backs, 10
Sofa table, *60*
Sonnenberg Collection, 14
Specimen marbles, *99, 302*
Spruce fir, 11
Stokes, James, 21, 22, *269*
Stonleigh Abbey, 17
Streatland Castle, *114*
Sunburst or sunray frame, *301*
Symonds, R. W., 13, 14, 15, 19n.1

Table, card, 77, *115*
Table, pier, *91, 95, 96, 99, 101, 105, 107, 109, 111, 121*
Table, sofa, *60*
Table, tray-top, *44*
Tapestry, Dublin, 15
Tax-free port of Dublin, 7
Teahan, John, 15
Temple, Sir John, *70*
Temple-Winthrop-Minot family, *70*
Thermometer, *113, 127*
To His Majesty, *125*
Trade, Early Federal, *146*
Travels Through England, 8, 17
Trinity Church, 9
Tyrone House, 18, *222*

United States, frigate, *146*

Van Rensselaer family, *271*
Venetian, *65*
Venetian craftsmen, 14
Venice, 14
Vessels from London, 12, 21
Victorian convex mirror, *299*
Victorian mirror plates, 10

Vile and Cobb, 15
Vile, William, 15
Virginia pine, 11

Wadsworth family, 19, *280*
Wall bracket, *193, 194, 195*
Walnut, American, 11
Washington commemorative mirror, *269*
Washington, G.-commemorative mirror, *270*
Washington, G., Esq.-commemorative mirror, *271*
"Washington" mirror, *154*
Waterford, 7, 8, *303, 304*
Waterford chandeliere in Independence Hall, 9
Waterford chandeliere in Trinity Church, 9
Waterford, exportations from, 7, 8, 9
Wayne and Biddle, 21, 22
Welsh counties, 23
West Indies, Irish glass exported to, 9
White pine, 11, *150*
Whiting, Stephen, 21
Wicklow, County, 14
Williamsburg, 8
Wilmerding, William, 21, 22, *319*
Wolseley, Lady, 10, 13
Woodbury, Luther, *174*